KOS

General Guide

KOS

JOHN BOWMAN

EFSTATHIADIS GROUP

ISBN: 960 226 211 7

Athens 1992

Printed and bound in Greece by
EFSTATHIADIS GROUP S.A.

Distributed by
EFSTATHIADIS GROUP S.A.
HEAD OFFICE: AGIOU ATHANASIOU ST. GR - 145 65 ANIXI ATTIKIS
TEL: (01) 8140602, 8140702 FAX: (01) 8142915 TELEX: 216176 EF
ATHENS BRANCH: 14 VALTETSIOU ST. GR - 106 80 ATHENS
TEL: (01) 3633319, 3614312, 3637284 FAX: (01) 3614312
ATHENS BOOKSHOP: 84 ACADEMIAS ST. TEL: 3637439
THESSALONIKI BRANCH: 4 C. CRISTALLI ST. ANTIGONIDON SQUARE
THESSALONIKI, GR - 546 30 TEL: (031) 511781, 542498, FAX 544759
THESSALONIKI BOOKSHOP: 14 ETHNIKIS AMINIS ST. TEL: (031) 278158

CONTENTS

1. Preface

The Dodecannese:
AN INTRODUCTION

An unusual word for an unusual locale. Many people, in fact, may not immediately recognize the word, although as soon as Rhodes is singled out, most people will respond positively. But this is ironic, since Rhodes was not actually a member of the original **Dodecannese,** while many people have quite specific links with two of the Dodecannese – **Kos** and **Patmos** – not to mention the fact that one of the roots of the word, **dodeka,** is one of the first Greek words everyone learns because it means "twelve", although in fact there are more than twelve islands in Dodecannese, which in any case were long known as the Southern **Sporades.** About the only thing that can simply be said is that they are a group of beautiful and interesting Greek islands in the eastern **Aegean.**

But to back up a bit and deal with the apparent paradoxes. The name of these islands, Dodecannese, means nothing more than "The Twelve Islands," but this term has no classical standing; indeed, it only was coined in 1908, when 12 islands that had enjoyed a "privileged" status under the Turks since the 16th century joined to protest the Turks withdrawal of certain privileges. Rhodes, Kos, and **Lipsoi,** now included in the Dodecannese, were not involved in this situation. But as their fate came to be entwined with the others in events following the Italo-Turkish war of 1911-12, these islands not only joined **"The Twelve";** Rhodes – always the largest and most influential island of this area – came to be the capital of the Greek administrative region, or Nome, now formally the Dodecannese. But there are 14 islands in the Nome that have independent local governments – **Rhodes, Telos, Syme, Chalki, Megisti, Kos, Nisyros, Karpathos, Kasos, Patmos, Lipsoi, Leros, Astypalaia,** and **Kalymnos** – (p.114,5, 130,1) while several of their dependent islets are also inhabited. As for the **Southern Sporades** – the latter word being Greek for "scattered islands" – this is seldom applied to any Aegean islands, at least by foreigners.

It is foreigners to whom this guide is primarily addressed, and whether this is the first visit to Greece or but one in many, this book is designed to make the Dodecannese as accessible and enjoyable as possible. Rhodes, of course, is one of the best-known "tourist spots" in the world, one of those distinctive places that has had centuries of experience

A view of the City of Kos with the harbour ▶ 9

in providing hospitality – and sunshine – for millions of visitors; before this guide is ended, it will have cast a fresh light on many of the old and new aspects of Rhodes. So, too, on Kos, home of the Sanctuary of **Aesclepius,** an ancient medical center, and of **Hippocrates,** the father of medicine and of the **Hippocratic Oath,** still taken by doctors many little-known points of interest. For there is far more to these islands than is often publicized. There are discos, to be sure, but there is also bicycle riding; there are beaches, but there are traditional costumes; there are chic boutiques but there are also sponges; there are Greek and Turkish remains, but there are also **Crusader** and Italian

A restaurant on the beach

in many lands. And on Patmos, as well, where St. John the Divine received and then dictated the **Revelation.**

But these are merely the most obvious attractions of the Dodecannese, and it is the aim of this guide to illuminate the tremendous diversity of these islands, even to reveal structures; there are bustling streets with souvenirs and grand hotels – even a casino, but there are remote villages following age-old patterns of life. All this and much more will be made accessible by this guide.

12

THE PHYSICAL ENVIRONMENT

Perhaps because these islands were never historically bound, but in any case because of their diversity, it makes more sense to provide the details of mythology, history, biography and such human dimensions under each individual island. But it is also true that the Dodecannese do share a geography, an environment, an ecology. And although not all visitors are interested in such matters in the abstract, they sooner or later must interact with these very real physical elements: if nothing else, the climate, the sea conditions, the terrain, the food and drink, all these are of immediate concern to even the most casual tourist.

FORMATION OF THE DODECANNESE ISLANDS

The ancients recounted various myths to explain the presence of individual islands such as Rhodes, but the modern geologist's explanation is in some ways even more intriguing. In this contemporary version, the formation of the Aegean world is a chapter in the larger story of the formation of the earth's major land and sea forms, one that goes back to at least 200,000,000 years ago. At that time there was a single mass of land on this planet; the land is now called Pangea and the surrounding sea is called Panthalassa (and thus do modern geologists pay tribute to the Greek mythological realm). A large bay extended across the area that would eventually become the Mediterranean, the Greek mainland, and all the way into the Middle East; this is now known as the Tethys Sea, and over millions of years great sediments were laid down over this sea's bottom (thus accounting for the fossils of marine organisms that may now be found on high land throughout the Aegean).

About 200,000,000 years ago, **Pangaea** began to break apart into two masses that in turn eventually split into the continents we know today. (This so-called drifting is explained by geologist's theory of plate tectonics.) All this took millions of years, during which time the **Tethys Sea** receded at its eastern end and became linked at the west to what became the Atlantic Ocean. By about 65,000,000 years ago the major movements had ceased and the shapes and locations of the continents were essentially those of our day. But the Aegean Sea and its islands still did not exist in their present forms; some scientists, in fact, believe that the entire Mediterranean Sea dried up at least a dozen times during this period as the water drained out into the Atlantic and then came 13 back as the continents of Africa and Europe continued to open and close near the Strait of Gibraltar. Meanwhile, as the great plates moved against one another, they pushed up the great mountains that border the Mediterranean Sea as well as those mountains that would eventually surface as the islands of the Mediterranean.

For eventually the Mediterranean Sea receded to its present level, leaving the shorelines and islands much as they are today. In the last million years, however, and even in quite recent times, there have been minor adjustments: earthquakes, volcanoes, local subsidence and elevation, delta formation, erosions – all have contributed to shaping the Aegean world. But the major forms of the Dodecannese are explained by their being peaks of the vast submarine massif that is linked to the continents of Europe and Asia. The

Bouganvilaea

Dodecannese are actually remnants of the range that extends down through Greece, the Peloponnesos, Crete and over to the Turkish mainland. Because the African plate is still pushing against the Aegean plate, the land at its edges is relatively unstable so that there are volcanic islands (such as **Santorini** and **Nisyros)** and occasional earthquakes. But the visitor need hardly worry about either of these phenomena: the last earthquake of any consequence in the Dodecannese was one on Kos in 1933, while the last major earthquake on Rhodes was in 1863.

Most of the Dodecannese, like the other Aegean islands, are composed of limestone, a sedimentary rock laid down over millions of years when the Tethys Sea covered the entire area; there is also some flysch, a sedimentary deposit largely of sandstone. None of the Dodecannese can claim either the fine marbles or other minerals and metals that are found on some of the other Aegean islands, although there are some good local building stones.

The total land area of the Dodecannese – the 14 major islands and their dependencies – is some 2,700 sq. km, or about 1,064 sq m. (To give some sense of this, Crete alone is some 8,300 sq. km.) Rhodes itself constitutes over half the area – some 1,450 sq. km.

AVERAGE MONTHLY TEMPERATURES
IN CENTIGRADE

	Atmospheric Air of:		Sea Surface (1400 hrs) at:	
Months	**Kos**	**Athens**	**Kos**	**Ierapetra Crete**
JAN	11.6	9.3	14.8	17.1
FEB	12.0	10.0	14.9	16.2
MAR	13.3	14.4	15.5	16.9
APR	16.6	15.5	17.9	17.9
MAY	20.6	20.2	21.0	20.0
JUNE	25.0	24.7	24.2	22.3
JULY	27.2	27.5	25.9	24.2
AUG	27.6	24.6	25.4	24.8
SEPT	24.9	24.6	24.9	24.2
OCT	20.4	18.8	20.4	22.5
NOV	16.4	14.9	16.4	19.6
DEC	13.2	11.1	13.2	17.4

THE CLIMATE OF
THE DODECANNESE

Although there is some slight variation in the weather on the Dodecannese – particularly in relation to the elevation – the islands generally enjoy a Mediterranean climate as defined by geographers, but with some sub-tropical elements. After all the technical details of the Mediterranean climate zone have been explained, it almost comes down to being one that will support olive trees, because what the olive tree needs is what the Dodecannese provide: hot, dry summers, clear if cool winters, and plenty of sunshine throughout the year. The Dodecannese boast of about 300 days when the sun can be seen. The summer is undeniably hot, but not the withering, enervating heat of the tropics. Winters can be cold at times,

Sunset

but not so cold nor so extended that they require the diversion of large resources or energy. At higher elevations, of course, conditions differ, but neither the olive nor tourists are apt to be found there. There is virtually never frost or snow to be found on the Dodecannese, at least at sea level, and the winter rains tend to come and go quickly.

What makes the islands especially comfortable in the hot summer months are the breezes that come at different times of day and usually make summer nights quite bearable. In fact, from July through September, the steady wind from the northeast, known in Greece as the **meltemi,** keeps the whole Aegean quite refre-

shed, and even short inter-island hops by sea can sometimes be rough.

The fact that the Aegean is relatively isolated from the major oceans' patterns means that the water temperature around the Dodecannese remains somewhat higher at the surface than at depths; in the winter, however, the lower depths "hold" the upper layers to relatively higher temperatures (than would be true in the open sea). This relatively higher and more consistent surface temperature of the Aegean accounts for the mild winter temperatures – both water and air. But there is no use pretending that any except the most rugged will care to swim in the Dodecannese between October and May.

On the Dodecannese there are no freshwater lakes and no rivers or streams worth mentioning with the exception of a few on Rhodes, but there are numerous springs and some seasonal torrents on the larger islands. Rainfall is generally light and concentrated in the few months between September and May. But Rhodes is exceptionally green and fertile, and Kos, Leros, and Karpathos are also well-watered and support considerable vegetation. On several smaller islands, fresh water is a challenge for the inhabitants but never presents much of a problem to visitors. And there are some thermal spings and baths on Kos and Kalymnos.

ANIMAL LIFE

Except for the omnipresent birds and insects, the only animal life most visitors will be aware of on the Dodecannese will be the domesticated variety – sheep, chickens, pigs (and even these will be most present when served up on restaurant plates). The same holds true for the fish, although a visit to certain seaside markets should prove interesting. (And don't forget that the sponge is actually what remains of a marine animal, not a plant). The one island that has any exceptional animal populations is Rhodes. In addition to the famous butterflies (see page 104), there are some unexpected birds such as vultures, jays, and jackdaws. There are deer now running wild in a few locales, but the Italians re-introduced them earlier in this century. There are some small mammals – hare, badgers, martens, and foxes; there are some snakes (including one small poisonous species, but the chances of a typical visitor running into one of these are virtually nil); there is also among the usual Mediterranean lizards one unusually large species, – 12-14 inches long – **Agama stellio,** sometimes called 'the Rhodes dragon' but actually a hardun that is common throughout the Nile Delta.

PLANT LIFE

The cultivated plant forms of the Dodecannese are the usual ones of the Mediterranean – the olive, the grape, the fig, wheat and some other cereal grains, all the familiar vegetables and fruits; the only unfamiliar ones to many visitors might be the carob trees, some tobacco grown on a couple of islands, the pistacchio trees of Rhodes, and a variety of lettuce from Kos. But the real delight, if not surprise, comes from the wild vegetation. The trees, again, are not that unexpected – the pines, cypress, juniper, holm oak, some chestnut: likewise, the basic ground-cover is the familiar **maquis** of much of the Mediterranean – the tough, 17

scrublike plants and evergreen shrubs, including thyme, broom cistus, mock privet, and so many other species. Some islands are really quite green and fertile – Rhodes and Kos, for instance – while others of the Dodecannese are quite arid and barren, but all can boast of some wildflowers. There are the anemones and poppies, the wild marguerites, fennel, chamomile, several orchids, and many bulbs and tubers such as crocus, gladiolus, sternbergia, and cyclamen; on higher ground are found such lovely specimens as lilies, honeysuckle, hawthorne, peonies, and primrose. But of the over 6.000 wildflower species known to grow in Greece, some are found mainly in the Dodecannese or on the Greek islands off the coast of Turkey – one such being the **Ferula chiliantha,** a close relative of the plant whose stems the Sicilians use to make "cane" furniture. There is the **Paeonia Rhodia** Stearn, for instance, a peony endemic to Rhodes. And there are plants such as the **Hyoscyamus aureus,** a henbane, and **Lithospermum fruticosum,** a shrubby gromwell, both found mostly on Rhodes and Crete. All in all, whether visitors simply enjoy the colourful flowers or wish to identify them, there are plenty of species throughout the Dodecannese to keep happy.

Scenes from the island of Kos

2. Visiting Dodecannese

WHEN WE GO

Although most people have relatively little choice when it comes to the time period for their vacation, there are two main factors that should be considered by anyone with any choice when considering the Dodecannese (and Greece in general). These two factors are clearly related: the weather and the crowds.

Weather: The Dodecannese, like most of Greece, boast of about 300 rain-free, sun-visible days a year, so avoiding long rainy spells or finding the sun is not the issue. To be sure, there is considerable variation throughout Greece as a whole – from Macedonia to Rhodes, say – and then again from sea-level locales to mountainous heights. But since most people stay close to the coast – and tend to concentrate in southern Greece – this is hardly the issue, either.

What must be stressed, rather, are (1) the fact that the Eastern Mediterranean and such islands as the Dodecannese are **not** in the tropics, and (2) the region is subject to occasional brisk winds. Because of the delightful climate that the Dodecannese enjoy for 6-8 months of the year, many people have the mistaken impression that they are like some tropical paradise: consult the chart on p. 15 ' to see what the average temperatures are throughout the year on Rhodes and you will see that both air and water cool down appreciably. The simple fact is that most people will not care to swim in the Dodecannese between October and May, and people looking for a sun-filled holiday will not find the islands much fun between November and March.

But if you are not seeking a holiday of the kind largerly spent on the beaches and in crowded cafes, these off-season months in the Dodecannese can be delightful. Spring is a relatively short season, but starting in March-April many flowers come into blossom and the air begins to warm. By June, in fact, the greens of the landscape begin to give way to browns and yellows – because of the sun-filled, rainless days so beloved by travelers – and there is often a dusty haze that settles over many of the islands. Not until October does the rain begin to bring back some of the green, and although the weather definitely cools down from November to March, it is not the bone-chilling cold of northern lands: the sun is seldom gone for long, clear blue skies are often present even if the air is a bit cool, and a light jacket allows you to move around. (A ship voyage on a cold winter's day, however, is something quite different.)

Then there are those winds. The Aegean from July to September is exposed to a fairly steady stream of air from the northeast, what the modern Greeks know as the **meltemi**. This prevailing wind help relieve what might be a quite oppressive heat during these months and generally refreshes, the atmosphere. But the meltemi also makes for fairly choppy seas on occasion: it comes of something as a surprise to many travelers throughout the Aegean that relatively short sea trips can be relatively rough. But all the people operating the ships know and respect these conditions and smaller boats simply don't put to sea when things are too rough.

Crowds: Since these weather conditions are generally known to those in the world of tourism, it is no coincidence that most people converge on the Dodecannese from June through July and August. And in more recent years, so many people have been trying to avoid these peak months that even May and September are fairly busy. But aside from the impact of such numbers of foreigners on the Dodecannese and their inhabitants, do such crowds really affect other visitors?

Decidedly yes! Fo one thing, they can definitely fill up all the hotels on such islands as Rhodes, Patmos, and Kos so if you are particu-lar about your room you must make advance reservations. Otherwise you might well have to stay in far less classy and far more remote hotels, or even in rooms in private homes – and although many of these can be quite comfortable and plea-sant, they may not be to everyone's taste. Young people probably won't care if they have to bed down once in awhile on a floor or bunk or even sit through the night on a cafe chair, but not everyone will go for this. So to repeat: for high season – say, June-July-August – on Rhodes, Kos, Patmos at least, make reservations in advance if you require particular accommodations.

As for food and drink, although the islands have never been known to run out of them, there is no denying that restaurants and cafes can become very crowded during the peak months. What this means is that you must often wait to be seated and served, that when service comes it is often hasty, and that often items on a menu are sold out. But again: no one goes hungry or thirsty.

Meanwhile, transportation facilities can also become crowded during these peak months. If you can afford 1st or 2nd class, you can probably avoid most of these situations. And many people who travel around the Greek islands find the crowds part of the pleasure. Even so, you might want to avoid certain especially crowded occasions: for instance, Easter weekend; on the days around August 15, when many Greeks make pilgrimages to Tinos and Paros; and near the end of August and early in September, when many people all head for Piraeus and Athens as the summer begins to close.

So where does this leave the visitor to the Dodecannese – and the Greek islands in general? If you come too early, not only will the water be too cold for swimming but many of the touristic facilities won't be operating – outdoor restaurants, for instance, may not have opened, archaeological sites and museums might be on reduced hours, there won't be

as many ships or planes to choose from. But the lack of crowds might well compensate for these, at least for some travelers. Furthermore, not all islands attract such crowds even in the peak season, so one possibility is simply to avoid such places as Rhodes, Kos or Patmos during the peak season – or at least pass through them during a day or so and go on to less crowded islands.

But in the end, you must go to the Dodecannese when you want to and you will find – and make – the holiday you want. Whenever you go, though, travel light, with as little luggage as possible, and you will find everything about your trip goes easier.

Windsurfing

TIME FOR
THE DODECANNESE

Some people's ideal Greek holiday is to see as many of the cities and sites and islands as possible within a set period of time; other people's ideal would be to spend three weeks lounging about Rhodes. Between such extremes would fall most people's ideal holiday. In any case, this guide can be used to make any of these ideals more possible and pleasant. As indicated elsewhere, much depends on the time, money, and energy you are willing to spend: thus, air travel to the more distant points obviously frees a lot of hours for sunbathing or sightseeing.

Here are some suggestions about how to use your time in the Dodecannese. It is assumed that you are setting out from Athens or Piraeus.

3-7 Days: Most people will probably want to head first to Rhodes: perhaps this is the occasion to indulge in an airplane ticket, as the ship passage consumes 18 hours **each way** (although many of those hours are during sleeping hours and saving you hotel fees). But with even 3-7 days on the islands themselves, you'd still have time for only about one or two others besides Rhodes: Kos and Patmos are the most obvious goals; Karpathos might be more interesting to some (and could be visited enroute to Crete); or go up to Kalymnos (and then straight on to other Aegean islands or Piraeus).

8-14 Days: Time enough to see several of the Dodecannese beyond Rhodes (3-4 days); Kos (2 days); Patmos (1 day); Karpathos (2 days); Kalymnos (2 days). Pick out a couple of the smaller and less frequented islands (from the descriptions that follow in this guide); if you combine ships' schedules, you can make your way along several routes and get on to Crete or Samos or even to some foreign port.

15+ Days: If you were determined to do so, you could probably see all of the 14 major Dodecannese in 15 or so days, but this wouldn't allow you much time to explore as a lot of your time would be spent on ships. Not every island can be gotten into and out of every day, so it would take a lot of careful planning to make sure you don't get stuck on one of the less exciting islands for a disproportionate amount of time.

Even the air links between Rhodes and Kos, Karpathos, and Kassos won't save you all that many hours. Better to select a half dozen islands that appeal to you and concentrate on these.

TRAVELING AROUND THE DODECANNESE

Traveling to and from and among the Dodecannese is both more easily accomplished, if more difficult to explain, than is generally realized. This section will explain these apparent contradictions. In particular, it will dispel one current traveler's tale: that you can't move around the Greek islands, including the Dodecannese, without constantly returning to Piraeus.

AIR

Most travelers in the Aegean will not be using the air service – whether because it is too expensive or too unromantic– but for those with more money than time air connections with the Dodecannese offer a definite convenience; consider that the ship passage from Piraeus to Rhodes requires a solid 18 hours, while flight time is barely 1 hour. As for the comparative costs, they change often from year to year that it is confusing to give actual figures; but it is fair to say that air fares are less than first class on the ships, anywhere from about twice to just one-quarter more than second class (as ship fares vary greatly) dependent on the type of ship, traffic volume, etc.), and from about

twice to three-quarters more than tourist class. Since people who travel first class tend not to worry about such costs, this may not be a factor; for others, what it means is that you end up paying about twice as much to get to some island while saving quite a few hours.

In any case, there are air connections to only a few of the Dodecannese. Except for charter flights to Rhodes – almost always part of package tours that require you to stay in particular hotels, etc. – there are no air links to cities outside Greece. The air links to the Dodecannese, therefore, are all by the Greek national airline, Olympic Airways; they all originate or end at the Athens-Hellinikon Airport, and actually most use Rhodes as the other terminus. There are about 5-6 flights daily each way between Athens and Rhodes.

There has also been one direct flight each way daily between Athens and Kos. Kos is also linked by Olympic to Rhodes. So, too, are Karpathos and Kassos linked to Rhodes. And Rhodes is also linked to Crete (Iraklion) by air. Once on Crete, you could make air connections with Santorini or Mykonos. But in general you cannot "fly around" the Dodecannese; even the links to Kos, Karpathos, and Kassos do not offer enough choices to allow you to get in and out on the most convenient schedules. On the other hand, in combination with the ship links, you can get around the Dodecannese using these air links.

As these schedules often change, and as many travel agents do not keep up with them, it is better not to try to make overly detailed plans from abroad; wait till you get to Greece, then go to the Olympic Airways or travel agent office, and plan your trip through the Dodecannese just before you are set to go.

SHIPS

From non-Greek ports: For most visitors this is not a possibility. But there are, in fact, several ways to get to the Dodecannese by ship from foreign ports. These are usually some ships that connect Rhodes to Alexandria, Egypt; Rhodes to Beirut, Lebanon, to Lattakia, Syria, and to Limassol, Cyprus; and there are even ships that connect Rhodes to Haifa, Israel, Dubrovnik, Yugoslavia, and to Venice, Italy. Such ships are not cheap, but they are certainly a delightful way of getting around the Mediterranean.

Then there are the cruise ships that might originate from some foreign port and put into at least Rhodes: but with only occasional exceptions, no one is allowed to leave these cruises and remain behind on the Greek islands. (For one thing, if you "jump ship," you won't have a proper passport clearance and you could have considerable trouble when you come to leave Greece.) There is the possibility that some freighter might be able to sell passage from one foreign port to one or another of the larger Dodecannese, but this would be an unusual situation. And of course privately owned or rented yachts may naturally sail into Greek waters and the Dodecannese ports. (Kos and Rhodes are the official ports of entry for passport and customs control).

Piraeus - Athens and the Dodecannese: Again, there are the cruise ships and yachts, but these will not answer most people's needs. Most people, rather, are simply interested in sailing direct from Piraeus to the Dodecannese. And there are indeed several possibilities. At least a couple times a week there has been one ship connecting direct to Rhodes. But there are other lines that go via other Greek islands and put in at Rhodes and other Dodecannese ports: one line has stopped at **Paros, Naxos, Ios, Santorini, Crete (Ayios Nikolaos** and **Sitia),** then at **Kassos** and **Karpathos** (including a second stop at Diafani), then on to **Halki,** the small island west of Rhodes, and finally on to Rhodes; another line goes via **Milos, Folegandros, Santorini, Crete** (Ayios Nikolaos and Sitia), and on to 25

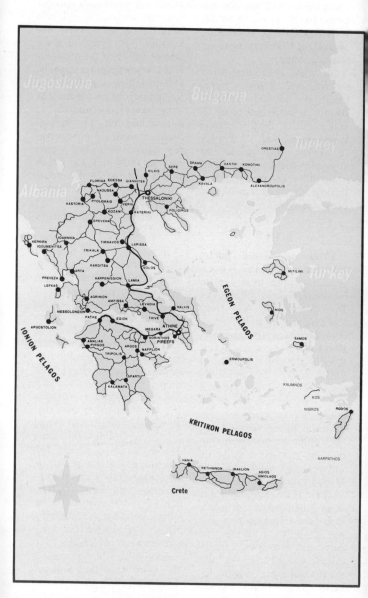

Patmos

Kassos, Karpathos (including Diafani), **Halki,** and **Rhodes;** still another line goes via **Tinos, Patmos, Leros, Kalymnos,** Kos, and on to Rhodes.

So it is relatively easy to get ships to and from Piraeus and the main islands of the Dodecannese. Schedules change frequently, fares keep increasing, it is often hard to find out precise details from abroad. But the ship links are there.

Other Greek Ports: As will be apparent from the previous section – on ship links between Piraeus and the Dodecannese – several of the Dodecannese are linked to one another as well as to other Greek islands. But in addition to those main lines, there are numerous smaller ship lines that operate between and among the Dodecannese islands themselves: ships between Rhodes and such islands as **Syme, Tilos, Nissyros, Kos, Kalymnos, Kastelorizo, Karpathos, Kassos, Halki, Leros, Patmos,** and still others. So once on one of the Dodecannese, you can usually get to the others by ship.

However, it is even more difficult to obtain precise and up-to-date information of schedules and fares about these ships when you are abroad – or for that matter in Athens. The National Tourist Organization has been known to issue weekly schedules and sometimes certain travel agents will be well informed. Best is simply to wait till you get to an island and then immediately ask the police or harbor master about ship connections. There's usually a local agent for the ship line, but be warned: they often will not volunteer information about competing lines and only grudgingly refer you to another agent. So keep your eyes and ears open while traveling the islands: other foreigners are often your best source of up-to-date information on these matters (because the local inhabitants, after all, are not that interested in island-hopping!)

Wild flowers of the Dodecannese

TRAVELLING ON THE DODECANNESE

The means of getting about on the various islands vary greatly from Rhodes to the smallest, but one way or another you will be able to get to anywhere you wish.

Here we discuss the general possibilities of the Dodecannese as a group.

PUBLIC BUS

All the major and sizeable Dodecannese have some public bus service – if only linking the main port to the main town: after all, the inhabitants have to get to and from ships, and often with large amounts of luggage. Not all the islands, however, can offer bus service to all the remote sites or monasteries, so you might have to walk a mile or two along a trail; also, schedules are not necessarily set for the convenience of the traveler who wants to spend a short time at a particular site and then move on. Thus some people might prefer one or another of the other possibilities discussed below.

TAXI

All except the smallest and least inhabited islands support at least a taxi, while the larger islands can provide quite adequate taxi service. For a small party anxious to see the more remote places in a minimum of time, a shared taxi is the best way to go. Or consider using a taxi in combination with the public bus when the latter's schedule is inconvenient. (For more about taxis, see that entry at Practical Information A to Z.)

CAR

Although it is possible to bring your own car on a ferry to many of the Dodecannese, it is a very expensive way to travel around these islands. Only a group of people intending to spend a fair amount of time traveling around Rhodes might find it economical – especially considering you have already paid to bring your car to Greece and might have to pay garage fees while on Rhodes.

Much more common is to rent a car – on Rhodes, that is. In recent years there has also been the possibility of renting a car on Kos and Kalymnos. Inquire when you get to Athens about the latest situation.

MOTORBIKE, SCOOTER, MOPED, BICYCLE

Increasing numbers of foreigners find these pleasant alternatives for getting around the islands, but it has only been Rhodes and Kos that 29

A restaurant at night

have commercial rental firms. Kos is especially known for its bicycle rentals.

BOATS

On Rhodes, Patmos, Kos, and several of the other islands, there are boats that go to either remote beaches or sites (such as a monastery or a sea cave) or to nearby islets; such excursion boats dock along the main harbors of the main ports and clearly adverti-se their services. Rates are reasonable and the excursion can become a pleasant way of spending some time with some fellow travelers.

WALKING/ HITCHHIKING

Walking obviously remains – the last resort for many but the first resort to some. Especially on the smallest islands and for the more remote locales, it may be the only way. Overland trails by being a destination closer than it might seem by main roads, but then again overland trails are not for everyone. Mean-while, hitchhiking (autostop) may appeal to some, but you cannot count on much traffic to the more remote locales.

ACTIVITIES & DIVERSIONS

Whether you head for the Dodecannese to see some particular historical or archaeological site or simply to enjoy the swimming and tavernas, there is much more to do on these islands than is generally known. We herewith offer some details about some of these possibly overlooked attractions of the Dodecannese.

SPORTS & OUTDOOR ACTIVITIES

For general remarks about sports and outdoor activities, look under these subjects in the section, "Practical Information A to Z": **Sports, Swimming, Underwater Sports, Yachting, Fishing, Hunting, Tennis.** Here we discuss aspects that apply more especially to the Dodecannese.

Swimming & Sunbathing: Swimming is a crucial element in the plans of many visitors to Greece so the section on "Swimming" (in Practical Information A to Z) should be read with special attention. It cannot be said too often: the water's temperature varies considerably from month to month (See Chart, p.15) and only the hardiest will want to swim in the waters around the Dodecannese between October and May. Only a few of the higher-class hotels on a few of the islands provide such amenities as changing rooms, showers, beach umbrellas, etc. And never underestimate the dangers of overexposure to the Aegean sun!

As for bathing or sunning in the nude, this has long been officially forbidden but unofficially overlooked, especially on several of the more isolated beaches tend to have a network

Windsurfing

Rowboating

of their own and keep informed of the possibilities. In any case, everyone should respect the local sensibilities as well as legalities.

As for the best of the beaches in the Dodecannese, these are identified and located on their respective islands in the accounts of specific islands.

Watersports: Except for a few of the expensive hotels on Rhodes and Kos, no one on the rest of the Dodecannese has been offering water-skiing, sail-surfing, paddleboats, or such activities (for hourly rates or fees). If you are determined to enjoy such sports, consult brochures of the best hotels and see what's available.

Underwater Swimming: Diving with SCUBA gear – portable oxygen apparatus – is forbidden on the Dodecannese (as throughout most of Gree-

ce) unless special permission is obtained. But snorkel gear – the tube, mask, and flippers – is allowed everywhere. Underwater swimming might be forbidden at special archaeological sites (and near any military installations): these would be posted, and obviously underwater photography would also be forbidden at such locales. When in doubt, check with the local police or the nearest office of the **National Tourist Organization.**

Tennis & Golf: There are tennis courts on Rhodes and Kos that visitors may use, and there is a golf course on Rhodes open to the public.

Boating: The Dodecannese offer many fine harbors and sheltered bays to those who would like to move about the islands either by sailboats or power yachts: it is always

32

Sunbathing

taken for granted that no one would be so foolish as to set out without the proper knowledge and experience. Although the farthest distance between any of the Dodecannese headlands may be less than 100 miles, the winds and waves of the eastern Mediterranean can be unexpectedly dangerous. Almost anything can be rented on Rhodes, but a more reasonable alternative for most people would be to take one of the day excursions on several of the islands, small boats that take groups to more isolated beaches or sites. (These are described at the respective accounts of these islands.) Both Kos and Rhodes, by the way, are official points of entry and departure for boats entering Greece (for customs and passport control, that is).

Fishing & Hunting: There is no freshwater fishing to speak of on the Dodecannese, but there is obviously a lot of saltwater fishing. Foreigners may fish without any licence, but they may not fish in waters used by professional-commercial fishers. Underwater fishers may use a speargun, but not within 100 yards of public beaches.

As for hunting – which does require a licence and observe seasons – it is unlikely that anyone would travel to the Dodecannese to hunt the few small birds and mammals.

Mountaineering & Walking: No one would head for the

Dodecannese for challenging climbs, but Rhodes boasts of one respectable mountain, **Mt. Atavyros,** 1,215 meters (about 4,000 feet) and this has one marked trail from the village of Empona to the peak. Karpathos also has two respectable peaks: **Mt. Lastos** (or **Kalolimni**), about 3675 feet high, and **Mt. Profitis Elias,** about 3325 feet high. But there are many opportunities for walks around any of the islands. Just be sure you have proper footwear, sun-protection, clothing for cool times, and sufficient water and nourishment. Remember, too, that most of the land (and its produce) usually belongs to private individuals: you walk on their lands as a guest.

FESTIVALS

The general remarks about HOLIDAYS (in Practical Information A to Z) should be read in conjunction with this section; there are listed the major national holidays of all Greece, and many if not all of these are observed on the Dodecannese with appropriate festivities. (It also means that most facilities are closed on these days, so you must make your plans accordingly). But in addition to these national holidays, there are many special holidays and festivals that are observed on one or several of the Dodecannese, sometimes with more intensity than elsewhere; some people might like to schedule their visits to the appropriate islands to take advantage of this. Listed here are the better-known of such occasions on the Dodecannese. If you are especially interested in such occasions, ask at the local offices of the police, the National Tourist Organization, or even travel agencies as soon as you arrive on an island; with luck you'll run into someone who is going to celebrate a nameday or a wedding or a baptism in some village, and you may be invited to come along. Till then, here are some special occasions to attend on specific Dodecannese.

Dancing the local dances

Jan. 6
Many coastal locales, harbors, etc.

Epiphany ("12th Night") is celebrated all over Greece with rites blessing the sea.

Feb-Mar
Carnival: Leros especially, but at many places.

Carnival is a movable occasion (dependent on Easter) and is observed with various festivities.

Mar-April
Easter: Patmos above all, but everywhere.

For 3-4 days, all of Greece gives itself **Easter.**

April-May
Kalymnos: Find out when the sponge fleet will depart and attend the ceremonies.

April-Oct
Rhodes: City Sound & Light performances (in alternating languages) are given at the **Palace of the Grand Masters.**

Jun-Oct
Rhodes: City Performances of traditional dances by the Nelly Dimoglou Folk Dance Troupe, one of the oldest and best in all Greece.

Jun 21
Rhodes: Kalafonon: St. John's Day is observed with bonfires.

July-Aug
Rhodes: Valley of the Butterflies. Thousands of butterflies gather here and tourists gather to see them.

July-Sep
Rhodes: Rodini In this suburb of Rhodes City there is an annual and popular wine festival; in addition to featuring samples of the wines of Rhodes, it offers many foods and gifts.

July 17
Leros & Kassos The feast of **Ayia Marina** is especially observed on these two islands.

July 20
Kastellorizo Ascents of the mountains peaks, lighting fires, feasting and dancing -- all to celebrate the Prophet Elias -- throughout Greece but especially here.

July 27
Kalymnos The feast of **Ayios Panteleimon.**

Aug 14-23
Rhodes: Kremasti combines athletic events with religious ceremonies for miraculous icon of Virgin Mary.

Aug 15
Patmos, Nisiros, Astipalea: Assumption, or Dormition, of **Virgin Mary** is observed throughout Greece, but especially on **Patmos** and these other islands.

Sept 14
Khalki: Moni Stavros Exaltation of the Cross: the rites bless crop seeds.

Nov 7-9
Syme: Monastery of **St. Michael Panormitis** Feast of the Archangel Michael attracts pilgrims from all over area.

TRADITIONAL POPULAR CULTURE

People have spent lifetimes trying to track down all the survivals of traditional and popular culture in the Greek world, but many visitors to the Dodecannese might be able to observe or participate in at least a few special occasions during even a limited stay. Here are some guideposts.

One of the best ways is to share in the traditional or special festivities listed on the calendar (p. 37). And even if you cannot time your visit to coincide with such events, there is always the possibility of attending a wedding or baptism or some such occasion when traditional music and dancing and feasting will play

a role. Some of the islands have special songs and dances, of course. Kalymnos is noted for its bagpipes **(tsambouna)** and its expressive songs; Nisiros keeps alive traditional folk music, especially at the weddings and dances of Perioli on August 15; on Kos, at **Patani,** a few kilometers from Kos town, a Turkish community still gathers to play traditional Turkish music; Rhodes City offers bouzouki music, plus dancing at its Wine Festival, as well as the professional folk-dance performances by the **Nelly Dimoglou** troupe. But music and dancing are seldom hard to come by anywhere in Greece.

Another approach for some might be to deliberately seek out those islands or villages where traditional ceremonies or traditions have been kept alive. Leros, for instance, observes Carnival in an unusual way: adults compose satirical verses that children dressed up as monks, recite at parties in homes where a marriage has occurred within the past year. (It is claimed that this can be traced back to ceremonies for **Dionysos** at Eleusis. The village of Olimbos on Karpathos is especially noted for maintaining its traditional clothes architectural style, a particular Doric dialect of Greek, and traditional costumes.

Those interested in traditional clothing, in fact, will have something of a festival of their own in the Dodecannese. In addition to Olimbos on Karpathos, where many of the inhabitants wear traditional clothing throughout the year, there is a town on Rhodes, Empona, where the inhabitants also wear traditional clothing everyday; and the women of **Tilos** wear traditional embroidered clothes much of the time; on Kassos, villagers wear traditional clothes on July 17, while those on Astipalea wear traditional clothing on August 15.

Yet another approach accessible to foreigners is to seek out every museum, collection, old house, or whatever that seems to have at least elements of the old and traditional. Lindos, on Rhodes, is usually passed through in a hurry by those on their way to its acropolis, but the town itself is a living museum of traditional medieval architecture. Rhodes City has the Papas Konstantinos House that is a museum of folk culture. Peek in old shops and you will often seek old textiles, ceramics, woodwork, metalwork, or such objects.

And if you are still determined to see more, inquire at the National Tourist Organization in each main city when you land on an island and someone should be able to direct you to any special locales or festivities. Remember, too, that many elements in the Orthodox Christian religion, especially as practices in the villages and countryside, can be traced to pre-Christian and pagan roots, so that you are experiencing a form of "living folklore" whenever you attend some religious occasion. If you speak Greek, of course, you will also be aware of how many traditional elements pervade the speech of Greeks – proverbs, superstitions, portents, catch phrases, and such. But the best way for most foreigners to share in the traditional culture of the Dodecannese is to attend some celebration or festival where music, dance, costumes, food, and various ceremonies all combine to present a true living folk culture.

PROFESSIONAL ENTERTAINTMENT

Those who need to be entertained by professional groups or individuals probably aren't travelling around the Dodecannese. But the fact is that the city of Rhodes does offer the Nelly Dimoglou Folk Dance Troupe, one of the oldest and finest in Greece, which performs between June and October; the city of Rhodes also offers a "Sound and Light" production from April to October. Professional musicians also pass through Rhodes and concertize on occasion. But that is about it for the Dodecannese. That still leaves discos or nightclubs with professional musicians and entertainers, and of course the movie theaters in large cities. And whether it is a sport or entertainment, there is the gambling casino in the city of Rhodes.

CRAFTS & SHOPPING

Most travelers through the Dodecannese, as elsewhere in Greece, look forward to taking

home some memento of this distinctive world, and there is no trouble finding shops that will sell you some souvenir. The problem is to find something that is truly indigenous and locally made. For the general problems of buying in Greece, see under SHOPPING & SOUVENIRS (in Practical Information A to Z); the Dodecannese present the same set of problems, especially when it comes to antiques. The best most visitors can hope for is a solid and tasteful and genuinely handmade object old or not.

There is one exception, however, to anything that is said about the Dodecannese: Rhodes. The city of Rhodes has been a magnet for so many tourists and travelers for so

long that its shops offer a dazzling selection of goods and gifts – probably the largest in Greece outside of Athens. But many of these items are not what most people come to the Dodecannese to purchase – tailor-made suits and dresses, expensive furs, jewelry, leather goods such as boots, even umbrellas and duty-free liquors. The main shopping district of Rhodes is a bazaar that should at least reward the window-shopper. But Rhodes does offer some indigenous goods: handmade carpets from Afandou, distinctive pottery and loomed textiles from Lindos.

So keep your judgment and wallet under control and you can find something to your taste. And follow the basic rules of souvenir-hunting throughout all of Greece: look around at first and get a sense of what's being offered at what prices, find something you like and can afford, then buy it and don't worry too much about its age – or source: a hardware store might have some item that appeals to you more than anything in the most expensive shop in Rhodes.

EATING & DRINKING

Since eating and drinking are among the principal diversions as well as basic necessities while traveling, you might as well take advantage of any of the specialities of the Dodecannese. The basic menu in these islands, of course, is that found throughout most of Greece (see "Food and Drink" in Practical Information A to Z) but there are some variations in the Dodecannese that visitors will want to sample.

Inevitably, fishes are among the pleasures of these islands. In particular, there is a kind of bouillabaise, or "fish stew," known as **plaki** that is sometimes found in restaurants of the Dodecannese. The islands also pride themeselves on their fine squid, or **kalamaria:** not everyone immediately takes to the idea of squid, but they are one of the pleasures of the Greek cuisine. Kos boasts of its excellent fresh fish – particularly its sinagrida, a seabream, and its **lithrini,** a small black fish. Leros boasts of its **marithes,** smelt; Kalymnos prides itself on its **ksifiyes,** swordfish, and **octopothi keftethes** – octopus meatballs! But almost any fresh fish grilled to order should prove a delight.

Try the fish with one of the local or at least Dodecannese wines. Rhodes boasts of its Lindos, a dry white, as well as of its Embona and Chevaliers de Rhodes. Kos, meanwhile, boasts of its Glafkos, its Tsirini, and its Theokritos.

Fresh fruits in season are another of the pleasures of

40

Two beautiful restaurants

41

Cleaning fish by the water

Fruitshop

variety of fruits that it proudly offers – figs, lemons, oranges, and pears among them.

Then there are the little unexpected treats: Kalymnos's main port, Pothia, offers a special sweet known as **Copenhai** (from Copenhagen). Leros puts caper leaves in saldas (claimed to be an aphrodisiac, if that interests you). And there will be other unfamiliar foods that appears on the menus throughout the Dodecannese. Having gone to all the trouble to come this far, you should try at least some of them.

travel throughout Greece. Kos is particularly proud of its watermelons, figs, cherries, bananas, and pomegranates; Kalymnos is proud of its tangerines, oranges, and figs; Rhodes, of course, has a

Repairing the nets

"Arghalios:" loom

Fishing

3. Kos

This slim little island – only some 110 square miles – has enjoyed a reputation far exceeding its size so that despite its remoteness it has attracted visitors from ancient times to the present. As so often in Greece, it is some classical historic and archaeological site that draws foreigners – in the case of Kos, the Asklepieion and its associations with Hippocrates – but once there it is the total environment, the experience of the place itself, that proves so engaging. Thus it is apt to be some quite unexpected element of your visit to Kos – the bizarre tree with "crutches," a bicycle excursion, Roman mosaics, a fish dinner by the harbor – that fixes this island in your memory.

TRAVELING TO
AND ON KOS

Ships and Airplanes to Kos: There is usually at least one ship daily in both directions – that is, coming to Kos from Rhodes or from some other island to the north or west (enroute to Piraeus or Samos), and thus departing in one or the other direction. So you can pretty much count on getting in and out of Kos at your own convenience. Meanwhile, O-lympic Airways provides daily flights to and from Athens, and usually four other flights a week between Rhodes.

Getting Around Kos: There are the usual choices of public buses, taxis, rented cars, and tour excursion buses, plus boats that take groups to remote beaches. But the "in"

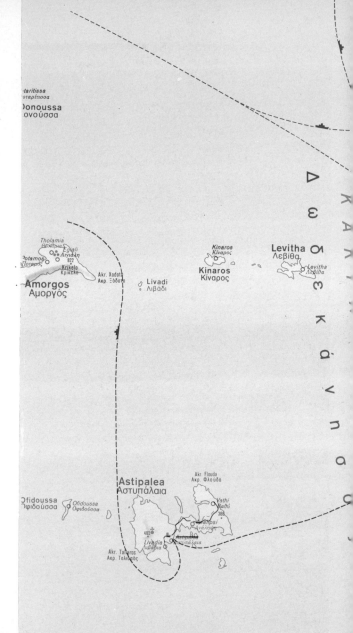

taritissa
οταρίτισσα

Donoussa
ονούσσα

Tholamia
Θολάμια
Egiali
Αιγιάλη
822
Potamos
Ποταμός
Krikelo
Κρίκελο

Akr. Xodoto
Ακρ. Ξόδοτο

Amorgos
Αμοργός

Livadi
Λιβάδι

Kinaros
Κίναρος

Kinaros
Κίναρος

Levitha
Λεβίθα

Levitha
Λεβίθα

Δ
ω
δ
ε
κ
ά
ν
η
σ
α

Astipalea
Αστυπάλαια

Akr. Flouda
Ακρ. Φλούδα

Vathi
Βαθύ
368

Ofidoussa
Οφιδούσσα

Ofidoussa
Οφιδούσσα

Analipsi
Ανάλημη

480

Livadia
Λιβάδια

Astipalea
Αστυπάλαια

Akr. Taloros
Ακρ. Τσλίψος

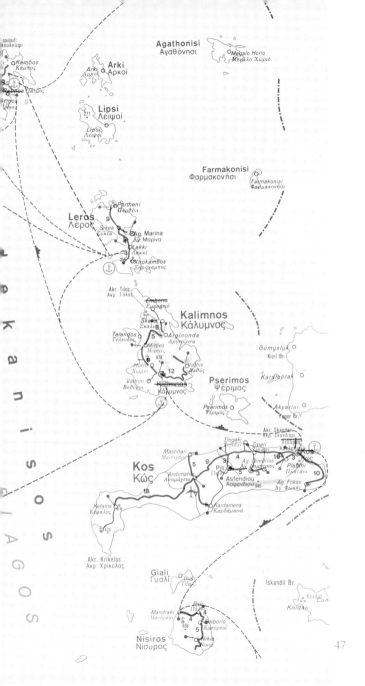

thing to do in Kos is to rent a bicycle (or moped, if you're so inclined): there are several shops in the main city of Kos. You can easily walk all around the city of Kos and most of its nearby sites, but the Asklepieion is about 3 miles away, just the right distance for a bicycle ride through the Greek country side.

ACCOMMODATIONS ON KOS

Hotels: There are dozens of hotels on Kos – ranging from Class A luxury resorts to the standard-but-decent Class C and then on down the line to basic rooms to rent in private homes. Most of the hotels are in and around the city of Kos, but there are increasing numbers of hotels springing up at beaches elsewhere around the island. Moreover, Kos, has now gone for the mass-market international tourist trade, so these new hotels offer many of the facilities that go with these resort complexes – tennis, mini-golf, discos, and such. It is not everyone's idea of a Greek island vacation, but they're here for those who want them.

Restaurants: Traditionally these have been the principal evening diversion for visitors to Kos – especially those down along the harbor of the old town. Fresh fish would be the prime choice, but there is the full Greek menu. And after you've eaten your fill, you traditionally move on to a cafe for a coffee and a sweet. Then a stroll around town and back to your hotel.

A BIT OF BACKGROUND

Probably everyone associates Hippocrates with Kos, but the island has a history that extends thousands of years on both sides of this notable. Kos, in fact, is one of the relatively few Greek islands known to have had Neolithic settlers; then in the Bronze Age Kos was settled by people from Caria, on the opposite coast of Asia Minor; the first known Greeks were Dorians (sent out from Epidauros, as it happens – but perhaps not so coincidental when later both places turn out to be centers of the cult of Asklepios). Kos never had much luck in choosing its allies, and during the Peloponnesian Wars was punished by both the Athenians and the Spartans. In 366 BC, its old capital – probably what is known as Astipalaia – was abandoned in favor of a new capital on the site of the present city of Kos. Clearly well sited to participate in the maritime commerce of this part of the Mediterranean, Kos now prospered and began to become widely known for its Asklepieion, or sanctuary dedicated to Asklepios, the hero and god of healing whose cult spread throughout much of the Greek world by the 4th century BC. On Kos, its prominence must have owed much to the island's claim to be the birthplace of Hippocrates (about 460 BC), for it was his ideas about illness and medicine that were generally said to be followed at the Asklepieion's school of medicine. Kos also could claim several other notables of this time – the poet Philetas, the bucolic poet Theocritus who lived for some time here, and the painter Apelles, who at least worked on Kos. It so happened, too, that Ptolemy II Philadelphus, son of the founder of the Ptolemies who took over a large part of Alexander's empire, was born on Kos in 308 BC. But none of this saved Kos from the fate of most of the Greek world: absorption into the Roman Empire, attacks by the Saracens, takeover by the Western Europeans – first the Genoese, and then from 1315 to 1522, the Knights of St. John of Rhodes – and then the long rule of the Turks. With the rest of the Dodecannese, Kos was taken over by the Italians in 1912, and did not get to join the modern Greek nation until 1947.

But for all this history, Kos today seems pleasantly low-keyed. There is, in fact, an almost tropical languor to the atmosphere of the island, perhaps due to the palm trees and flowering bushes that surround you in the city of Kos and the generally relaxed pace

One of many beautiful restaurants on the island

compared to such cities as Rhodes or Iraklion. The island is well watered and quite fertile, so it produces plenty of fresh fruits, cereal grains, vegetables, olives, and even some tobacco. It is fairly mountainous, with its highest peak, Mt. Oromedon (or Dikaios), rising to some 2780 feet. It is only 7 miles at its widest point. and there is only one harbor worth speaking of, that at Kos, at the northeast tip of the island. Note, too, that the Turkish Peninsula of Bodrum (or Halikarnassus) is only some 3 miles to the north of this tip, while the Turkish Peninsula of Knidos is some 10 miles to the south.

THE CITY OF KOS

The capital and port of the island, Kos is an unusual mixture of the old and new; although founded on this site in 366 BC, the city has suffered a series of major earthquakes so that its ancient remains 49

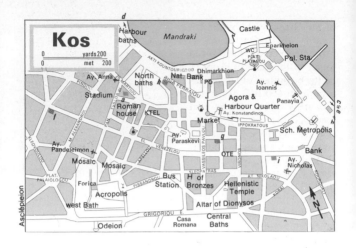

Kos

were often incorporated in subsequent reconstructions. And after the last of these earthquakes – April 23, 1933 – the town deliberately rebuilt itself in a modest manner to minimize the damage from any future earthquake. But there are plenty of things to see and do in and around Kos, and it is a delightful city just to stroll around, with its many gardens and trees, its unexpected archaeological sites, its great Castle of the Knights, and its various Turkish structures. (Of the 11833 inhabitants only 1100 or 9.3% are still said to be Moslems).

The first goal for most visitors will probably be the so-called **plane tree of Hippocrates;** its rotting trunk is about 45 feet in diameter, and its branches extend out only to be propped up by columns and piles of ancient marble and

wooden "crutches": all very strange, even if the tree is only at most 500 years old and could by no means have been used by Hippocrates to teach under. Off to the side of this square is the **Mosque of Gazi Hassan Pasha,** or Mosque of the Loggia with its elegant minaret; the mosque dates from 1786, and there is a staircase up to the second floor. An adjacent fountain uses an ancient sarcophagus for its basin.

On the seaward side of the square sits the **Castle of the Knights,** approached by a stone bridge over the old moat. It is really two castles, the first one having been built between 1450-1478; then, after the Turks attacked that in 1480, a second wall, or enceinte, was added between 1495-1514. Both incorporate stone from the Asklepieion and

Ancient remains   *Old walls*

Asklepieion

The Agora

Modified Corinthian Columns in the Asclepieion

other ancient structures on Kos. The entire castle is a classic of its era, with its bastions, towers, battlements, and other elements of military architecture; all around it, too, are inscriptions, escutcheons, and symbols of the Knights. There is also a small Antiquarium with some ancient remains. You can also obtain a good view over the harbor.

South of the castle and the tree square, you enter the area known as the **Khorio** – the walled town of the Knights, built on the site of the ancient harbor quarter and agora. It includes various remains from the Hellenistic Roman period of Kos, the most recognizable being the 8 columns (re-erected) with their acanthus capitals, from the Stoa of the

4th-3rd centuries BC. Most visitors will be content to wander through this extensive site just to marvel at both the extent and transience of the Roman Empire.

You will want to leave this area by the northwest corner, up near where you entered, and through a large stone gate that brings you into the **Plateia Eleftherias** (Liberty Square),

the heart of the modern city. Off to the left is the Defterdar Mosque, dating from the 18th century, but most people will head for the Museum, in a modern building. (It keeps limited hours and charges a modest admission). Hardly a world-class collection, but it has some interesting sculpture from the Hellenistic and Roman periods, including statues

of Diana of Ephesus and a statue of Hippocrates, possibly dating back to the 4th century BC.

On the southern edge of town, proceeding down Othos Pavlou to Leoforos Grigouriou, you would come to the old Roman baths and a fine Casa Romana; dating from the 3rd century AD, it has been largely rebuilt by the Italians in this century with the understandable aim of protecting to sit at this remote, provincial theater and gaze out over the landscape. Nearby is the Church of Ioannis Prodromos, left over from one of the earliest Christian churches on Kos.

Across the avenue from the Odeion is a major set of remains from the Hellenistic and Roman periods, now somewhat below ground level. Even if you are not interested in chasing down every old

General view of the City of Cos

the superb suite of mosaics: worth exerting yourself to see. And just a few blocks farther west is the Hellenistic, Odeion, once an enclosed theater; now seven of the original 14 rows of marble seats are still to be seen; you approach this theater along a cypress-lined avenue, and if you have come there at the right time of evening, it can be a most moving experience stone, a stroll through these excavations will reward you with their superb mosaics – all now protected but viewable by the public. There is also the Roman Baths with its calidarium ("heating chamber") almost intact; the frigidarium "cooling chamber") has been incorporated into a Christian basilica, of which various elements remain. You can also

The entrance to the harbour

walk along a well preserved Roman "main street," or **cardo.** Rising above the site is the old acropolis, now marked by a minaret; you can make your way up there by a flight of stairs and then wind through back streets to the center of town.

Well, there are numerous other ancient remains scattered around the town of Kos, mostly Hellenistic or Roman. (A bit west of Liberty Square, for instance, are some remains of the ancient Stadium, with its unusual starting gate.) But even if you do not choose to seek out all these remains, just walking around Kos is a pleasure. You will then enjoy all the more settling down at some cafe or restaurant down along the Mandraki ("sheep-fold") as the old harbor is called, looking at the yachts in the foreground, with their flags from many countries, while at night you may look off to the distance and see the lights from Asia Minor. It is just what Greek island travelling is all about

THE ASKLEPIEION

But one site should be visited by everyone, not so much because the remains are all that impressive but because of its historical associations: the Sanctuary of Asklepios. It is barely 3 miles from the center of town so it could even be approached on foot – as the ancients must have, after they came ashore; if that seems to be overdoing it, rent a bicycle – 57 it's done all the time, even by people who haven't been on one in years. The road is usually well marked, but just in case, take the left fork at the edge of town, and head for Ghermi, or Platanion.

The cult of Asklepios goes far back into the mists of Greek history, so far that the authorities still can't decide whether he was initially regarded as a hero or a god. (In the Iliad, he seems to be an ordinary mortal, "the blameless physician.") Nor can it be agreed as to where the cult began. But two things seem certain: Asklepios was always associated with healing and by about 500 BC Epidauros was making itself the center of his cult. From Epidauros the cult spread to places such as Athens – and Kos. The cult was perpetuated by the Asklepiadai, a secret fraternity of priest-doctors, and to establish a new shrine they always brought a sacred snake from the "mother" shrine at Epidauros. Asklepios would usually be represented with a snake, and that often coiled

Palm-tree shaded Avenues

Palace of the Regent

around a staff. The cult had its own festivals, hymns, processions, and sacrifices, and its increasing popularity in the years after about 400 BC seems to reflect the emergence of new generations of individuals seeking a more personal religion outside the more formal state religion. (Perhaps it might be thought of like the various Protestant sects that sprang up in the 19th century.)

At Kos, the cult almost from the first overlapped the importance assigned to the island's

native son, Hippocrates: he may have been little more than one of the Asklepiadai, or priest-doctors, but he seems to have imposed his own approach to healing on the Asklepieion of Kos. Or rather his followers did, for Hippocrates had evidently died early in the 4th century, before the Asklepieion of Kos really assumed its central role. At other Asklepieions, such as at Epidauros, cures seemed to have been largely effected by autosuggestion – really forms of faith-healing. But at Kos, the physician-priests seem to have taken a more "scientific" approach, using diet, baths, and exercise. So it was that people from all over the Greek – and later Roman – world would come to the Asklepieion as moderns might go to some great bath-spa or medical center. And so it was, that the Asklepieion became a place of great wealth and architecture, thriving in the Hellenistic Age under the Ptolemies and then under the Romans thanks to the patronage of such as Nero. But during the 6th century AD, the great Asklepieion seems to have been abruptly devastated – whether by an earthquake or marauders it is not known. By the time the Knights of St John came along in the 14th century, they treated the site as a quarry for ready-cut stone. Systematic excavation began early in the 20th century under the Germans, and was then continued by the Italians. More recently, there have been announcements of plans to establish a major international medical center beside the site – to carry on the ideals of Hippocrates.

Some of the many medical texts ascribed to Hippocrates do, indeed, sound surprisingly modern, but to be honest, none of the texts can be authoritatively established to have been written by Hippocrates of Kos – and in any case, there are so many of them that they end up being inconsistent. Included among the texts is the famed Hippocratic Oath, which was apparently like a contract made between a master physician and his apprentices. It still has no legal standing, but it remains in many lands as a statement of the highest ideals of the physician. You may never have thought of it this way, but every time you go to your doctor, you are paying your respects to Kos.

At the site itself, you may be overwhelmed by the sheer extent of the ruins – and restorations (for the Italians indulged in a fair amount of re-erections). Just walk through and up and enjoy what you see in the spirit of the place. You pass the Roman Baths on your left as you approach the lower terrace, which was surrounded by porticoes on three sides; the Asklepian Festivals were probably celebrated here. Along the fourth side is the retaining

Odeion of the City of Cos

Asklepieion

wall of the next terrace; near its center is a still functioning fountain and some reservoirs fed by pipes from the nearby sulfurous and ferruginous springs that were part of the cure offered here. You then proceed up the staircase in the center to the Middle Terrace, and immediately on the right see a fine little Ionic temple from about 300 BC; it was once decorated with paintings by the famous Apelles, but Augustus took these to Rome. In front of this temple is the great altar, with its own staircase; between the columns of its portico were once statues of Asklepios, his daughter Hygieia, and other members of his family. To the left of this altar are remains of a Roman temple.

Finally, you will climb the large staircase to the upper terrace, dominated by the Temple of Asklepios; in the Doric style, it is notable for its black marble lower base and the black limenstone threshold of the pronaos; a Christian

The harbour of Cos

chapel was at one point installed within, but only its altar remains. But the true reward for having come this far is the view, with the town of Kos lying in the middle distance, the Greek islands of Kalymnos and Pserimos to the northwest, and the great peninsuals of Turkish Asia Minor off to the east – Bodrum (or Halikarnassus) to the north, and Knidos to the south.

OTHER EXCURSIONS ON KOS

For most visitors, Kos town and the Asklepieion will probably be it, but the island actually offers several more points of interest. From Kos town to the farthest western point of the island is only some 30 miles, but the hilly roads put this out of reach of most cyclists. Public buses or taxis will be most visitors' preferred means, and there has usually been one bus that allows you

to make the roundtrip in one (long) day.

Your final destination is the village of Kefalos, and to get there you ride length of the island, with a number of possible stops and sidetrips. You leave Kos town by the same road as for the Asklepieion, but take the right fork; as you pass by the Asklepieion, you now get a good view of Mt. Oromedon, which rises behind it; there are several springs on this mountain, one of which still supplies the town of Kos with its water and was known to the ancients as **Vourina,** the Sacred Spring of Theocritus's 7th Idyll. At

Modified Corinthian Columns

about 6 miles, you pass through Zipari, with its early Byzantine basilica dedicated to St. Paul (some mosaics to be seen); a turnoff to the left would take you to the charming village of **Asfendiou:** this sits on the slopes of Mt. Oromedon's highest peak (2780 ft), Dikaios, which could be ascended from Asfendiou. Continuing on the main road from Zipari, you pass a ruined Roman agueduct and come into **Pili** (at about 10 miles); a trail from here leads (after 2 1/2 miles) to Palaio Pylai, once some ancient settlement but more importantly a Byzantine town; there are remains of the Byzantine castle and church (the latter with 14th-

Picking out post-Cards

century frescoes). The road from Pili then goes down to the southeastern coast to **Kardamaina,** known for its melons, pottery, and tomato juice; there are also some few remains of a Hellenistic theater and early Byzantine basilica; hotels and rooms to rent allow for an extended stay here, and the fresh-fish tavernas make that enjoyable.

Continuing on via the main road, you come (at about 16 miles) to **Andimakhia;** nearby is the airport, while a trail leads (in 2 miles) to what is left of the medieval Castle, erected by the Knights of St. John. Continuing on, the road comes down onto the coast of the Bay of Kamares – in which you'll spot the Rock of St. Nicholas – and at about 27 miles, you'll pull into **Kephalos;** there is a fine beach here and various tavernas; on a nearby slope is another castle, while at a locale known as **Palatia** are remains said to be those of the ancient capital of Kos, Astipalea. And if you are prepared to go all the way to the southernmost end of the island, you would see Hellenistic remains – two temples and a theater – and a Byzantine basilica. Most people will settle for the views from Kephalos.

So this would be about all of Kos that most people will get to see. There are a couple of other attractive fishing villages – Marmari and Mastihari – and a fine beach at Tingaki, about 8 miles out of Kos town.

But whether for 2 days or 20, you will find a visit to Kos offers relaxation – still the best cure for many modern ailments.

KALYMNOS

This relatively small (some 42 square miles) and remote island long enjoyed the unique distinction of being the sponge capital of the Western World. If it can no longer lay undisputed claim to this, the chief activity of Kalymnos does remain centered around sponges, and this results in a double bonus, so to speak, for those who take the trouble to visit this member of the Dodecannese: it is **not** an island self-consciously geared to tourism and it **is** an island geared to an age-old activity most of us will never again get a chance to experience.

Kalymnos can be reached by the small ships that make their way to and from Rhodes – although not all of these put in at Kalymnos – about four times a week, in each direction. It is also possible to take a day excursion boat from Kos. Most of the island's activities occur in its main port and capital, **Pothia,** but if you want to get around the island there are buses and taxis. And although, as mentioned, the island has not turned itself over to tourism, if offers several fine hotels – several at such delightful beaches as Mirties, Massouri, and Lina-

Fisherman "on the job"

ria. Its terrain is largely mountainous, but the islanders cultivate every possible valley and pride themselves on their various fruits – figs, tangerines, oranges and as well as their own olives and grapes. (Their once famed honey is no longer so evident.) Not surprisingly, the island is also famous for its seafood – particularly octopus meatballs, fried squid, and swordfish. The inhabitants, being independent and international in their sponge fishing affairs, have throughout history taken independent steps – painting their homes in the blue-and-white colors of the Greek flag to express their resentment at their Italian occupiers, and virtually deserting the island during World War II so as to avoid the Italian-German occupation and carry on the fight from abroad. But Kalymniots also keep alive many traditional ways – music, dances, and festivals, many of them associated with the comings and goings of the sponge fishermen.

Pothia

Everyone will arrive at the harbor of **Pothia** – and probably be struck by its "stage-set" appearance: its homes and buildings rise in ranks around the amphitheater-like harbor, and they are all painted in shades of blue, green, yellow, or brown. The buildings come to a quite abrupt stop, and then the barren slopes rise above the city; off in the distance you can make out the ruins of the medieval castle. Some 9000 of the island's total population of 13,000 live in or close by Pothia, and it can be quite a bustling town – especially in the spring, before the sponge fleet sets out, and in the autumn, after the sponge fleet has returned. There are hotels and restaurants, of course; there is even a little Archaeological Museum with finds from the island's long past; of more interest to many will be the Church of Ayios Sotiras right down on the seashore, with its frescoes and ikons and in particular its ikonostasis carved by Gianoulis Halepas.

Unless your Greek is pretty fluent, you will probably not get to hear the full story of what has happened to Kalymnos's preeminence in the sponge world. For centuries, Kalymniots dominated the sponge-fishing in the eastern Mediterranean – both as the divers for the sponges and as the processers (sponges must be cleaned in acid baths) and then as exporters and sellers. But two things began to challenge this tidy monopoly in the 20th century: the spongefishermen had to go farther away from Kalymnos to find enough sponges (because they had overfished their home-grounds) and the general exodus of Greeks took many Kalymniots to Tarpon Springs, Florida. But Kalymnos continued to be at the center of the Western world's sponge trade, because its fishermen found other rich sponge fields off Libya or elsewhere around the Mediterranean; meanwhile, the Kalymniots and other Dodecannese Greeks in Florida tended to cooperate with their relatives in the Old World, coordinating production and prices and effectively dividing up the markets in the West. In the 1970s, two new forces began to upset this neat arrangement: the rise in fuel prices (and eventually in all other costs, including interest rates) and Qaddafi's banning of the Greeks from Libya's offshore fields. The final blow came in the early 1980s, when Cubans in Florida began to exploit the rich spongefields off the Florida Keys and completely undersell the Greeks – not only in America but in Europe. (The final ignominy has been that a Kalymniot based in Paris became the exclusive importer of Cuban sponges into Europe – and Cubans began to appear on Kalymnos to sell Florida sponges to the Kalymniots!)

But as can only be said of so many of the Greek islands: they've seen worse in the last 4000 years. Meanwhile, spongefishing and processing

and selling remains the island's main activity. Even if you cannot be on Kalymnos just as the fleet leaves – sometime after Easter – or returns (about October), you can see something of the processing, for that goes on almost continually.

EXCURSIONS FROM POTHIA

Less than one mile southeast of Pothia is **Thermapighies,** with its radioactive springs; its waters are supposed to aid sufferers from arthritis, rheumatism, and digestive orders, but the bath has only modest accommodations and has never attracted a large following. You might prefer to take a boat excursion (about 40 minutes one way) to the **Cave of Kefalas** on the southern end of the island; it has impressive stalactites and stalagmites, and was once a sanctuary for worshippers of Olympian Zeus Or another little excursion might be to the convent on the

A monument by the harbour

hill above Pothia, where the nuns display the skull of their founder, St. Sabbas, in a coffin with a glass top. (After this you'll enjoy the view even more.)

A trip (via bus or taxi) to Panormos and Mirties on the west shores leads past the ruined Castle of the Knights to **Khorio,** the old capital of Kalymnos; another Castle sits above it. Proceeding out of Khorio, near Damos, you pass the remains of the Church of Christ of Jerusalem, built near the end of the 4th century; near this are ruins of a theater and a temple of Apollo as well as rock tombs (said to go back to the Mycenaean period); also nearby are the monasteries of Evangelistria and Ayia Ekaterii (which have traditionally taken in guests). Panormos and Mirties (which are only some 4 miles from Pothia) offer hotels and swimming.

An excursion in the other direction, to Vathy on the east coast, takes you past the entrance to the **Grotto of**

Another part of the town

Daskaleios, down on the inlet: you'd have to go there with an experienced boatman, but if you're interested in such sites, it's quite impressive – its main chamber being some 82 feet long. Vathy is made up of three villages, one of which, Rhina, serves as the port; the valley of Vathy is rich in both fruit and olive trees and in unexplored antiquities.

Two other possible excursions from Kalymnos are two small offshore islets, both offering unspoiled beaches. One is **Telendos,** off the northwest coast; it has ancient Greek and Roman remains as well as ruins of a medieval monastery and castle (with sunken remains of the medieval settlement visible offshore). And in the channel between Kalymnos and Kos is **Pserimos;** it is inhabited and also has a monastery.

NISYROS

Like Tilos, Nisyros is a port of call for the steamships – about twice a week, in each direction – going between Rhodes and Kos, but there has usually been a one-day excursion boat from Kos. And when was the last time you set foot on what is little more than an extinct volcano arising right out of the sea? Only some 15 square miles in area, Nisyros seems considerably larger because of the cone of some 2270 feet at more or less the center of the islet. No need to worry about an eruption, although there are still some active hot sulfurous springs – and even a little "spa" at Loutra. (An excurison truck takes visitors to the crater to experience the fumes and mud.)

Boats put in at the harbor and capital, Mandraki, above which sits yet another castle of

Two beach restaurants

the Knights, within which is the Monastery of Panayia Spiliani. In its administrative building and public school are some sculptures and ceramics from the Hellenistic and Roman periods as well as inscriptions and Byzantine icons. About a 1/2 mile from the town are remains of the ancient acropolis, with some well-preserved pre-classical walls.

There are only three other villages on Nisyros to speak of. Nikia is usually considered to be the loveliest, clinging to the edge of the old volcano's crater and offering a superb vista; it also has a monastery of St. John. Emborio is also

The Bronze statue of a Muse

A beautiful beach on the ilsand of Calymnos

well situated and has an old Byzantine fort. The fishing village of Pali has some sulfurous baths and a lovely clear beach.

But the most unusual feature of Nisyros is the celebration that marks August 15, the Assumption of the Virgin; the entire island marks this with folk music and traditional dances, while the Monastery of Panayia Spiliani at Mandraki serves a special hot bean soup. Nisyros is also noted for its traditional wedding ceremonies, in particular a dance called the "Perioli".

4. General Practical Information from A to Z

AIR TRAVEL

Within Greece, this is a monopoly of **Olympic Airways,** the national airline. **Olympic** has an excellent safety record. Almost all its flights originate in **Athens,** but there are some connecting routes (such as **Rhodes** and Crete in the tourist season). **Olympic** services all the major and more remote cities and islands of Greece with a variety of aircraft. During the tourist season, tremendous demands are placed on the service by the great numbers of foreigners, so you are advised to make reservations as far in advance as possible. You must be prepared for seasonal changes in schedules, too; and travel agents abroad will not always be up to date, so check your flights immediately upon arriving in Greece. Passengers who initiate their flights within Greece-may be limited to 15 kilos of luggage free of charge; those connecting with flights from abroad are allowed the international limits.

All Olympic flights, both international and domestic, operate out of the **West Air Terminal of Athens' Hellinikon Airport**; all other airlines use the **East Air Terminal.** The two are connected by frequent bus service, but about 45 minutes must be allowed to move from one to the other. Olympic also provides bus service from all its airports for a modest fee, but some people may find the wait not worth the money; especially if you are with a small group, a taxi can be relatively cheap. In **Athens** itself, the intown terminal for buses to and from the airport its too far from the center to walk there with luggage, but it is still considerably cheaper to take a taxi to this terminal and then the bus to the airport.

ALPHABET: See GREEK LANGUAGE

ANTIQUITIES: Greece enforces a very strict law against exporting antiques and antiquities. Anything dating from before 1830 is technically an antique and cannot be exported without official permission. This might be hard to prove in the case of a piece of textile or old jewelry, but the authorities are really interested in stopping the export of such items as ikons or manuscripts. As for genuine antiquities, small items are sold by several legitimate dealers, but permission for export must be obtained: the dealers should be able to direct you to the proper government office (which has traditionally been at the **National Archaeological Service, Leoforos Vassilissis Sofias 22, Athens**). Be wary of buying anything "under the counter": if it's not genuine, you're being cheated, and if it is genuine you're apt to find yourself in trouble.

AUTOMOBILE CLUB: Greece has a privately supported automobile club or association with offices in all main cities. Its Greek name forms the acronym **ELPA,** by which it is known; it means **Hellenic**

74

Touring and Automobile Club. Its head office is in **Athens** at the **Pyrgos Athinon** (corner of **Vassilissis Sofias** and **Mesogeion Ave**). It can assist you in obtaining an **International Driver's license** (so long as you have a valid license-which in practice is often accepted) or provide advice about insurance or other matters. For its members, **ELPA** provides a range of services, and its emergency repair vehicles will usually stop for any vehicle along the highway.

BABYSITTERS: Greeks have traditionally relied on their "extended families" to perform babysitting, but in recent years-due primarily to the needs of foreigners-Greek women have taken up this chore for money. They are not especially cheap, relative to wages in Greece and elsewhere, but they perform a necessary service. If you need a babysitter, contact the hotel reception desk, the **Tourist Police,** a travel agency, or the **National Tourist Information office.** The higher grade hotels should almost certainly be able to provide someone.

BANKS: There is no shortage of banks in Greek cities. Their normal hours are 8 AM to 2 PM, Monday through Friday, and some open for at least foreign exchange on Saturday mornings, Sunday morning and late afternoon or early evening. But banks do close on the main Greek holidays (See HOLIDAYS), so make sure you do not leave vital transactions to those days. Most goodsized banks maintain separate counters or windows for foreign exchange so be sure you get in the right line. Banks officially-and generally in practice do-give the best exchange rate (and usually give a slightly better rate for travelers' checks than for foreign currency). If you have bought too many Drachmas and want to buy back your own currency, you must provide the receipts of the Drachma purchases, and even so you will be limited as to how much you can convert back. You may be asked for your passport in any bank transactions, so have it with you. See also MONEY.

BARBERS: There are plenty of barbers in Greece, and you shouldn't need much language to get what you want. It is customary to tip the barber about 10%; if he uses a boy for cleaning up, you give him a few extra Drachma. See also HAIRDRESSERS.

BATHING: See SWIMMING

BICYCLES FOR RENT: Bicycles may be rented-usually from renters of motorbikes, motorscooters, etc.-in the main cities and resort centers. Rates vary, but they obviously become cheaper over longer periods. And if you are planning on renting for a specific trip on a specific occasion, reserve in advance, especially during the main tourist season. See also MOTORBIKES FOR RENT

BUS TRAVEL: There is frequent public bus service both within all large Greek cities and connecting main cities to smaller villages. In the cities, you pay as you get on the bus at the rear; keep your receipt for possible inspection. For intercity travel, you usually buy the ticket at the starting point; the ticket may include a numbered seat-but Greeks often pay little attention to this. However, especially during the main tourist season, buses can quickly become crowded, so you are advised to buy your ticket as soon as possible. Schedules between main cities and outlying villages have usually been set up for the convenience of villagers who need to come into the city early in the morning and return home late afternoon, so tourists may have to plan around such schedules. If you want to get a bus at a stop along its route, be sure that you signal clearly to the approaching driver, who may not otherwise stop.

CAMPING: Officially there is no longer camping in Greece except at the locales set aside either for government or commercial campsites. The **National Tourist Organization** has a brochure listing all such places around Greece. Such campsites, like those elsewhere, offer a range of support services, from hot water to electric outlets to food. Unofficially, there is still some camping-whether in vehicles or tents-on various beaches and fields. If you do try this, at least respect the property and dispose of all your wastes in approved ways. If you didn't stay too long in one place and picked fairly remote locales, you might get away with such camping.

CAR RENTAL: There are many firms that rent cars-both the wellknown international agencies such as **Hertz** and **Avis** and many locally owned firms-in all the large cities and resort centers around Greece. Rates are generally controlled by law, and variations are supposed to reflect different services, etc. The bigger international agencies, for example, can offer pickups and dropoffs at airports; they are also better equipped to provide quick replacement vehicles should something go wrong. Actual rates vary greatly depending on the size of vehicle, length of time, etc. You will find that it is much easier to rent a car if you have a charge card; otherwise you must leave a large deposit. You will probably want to pay the extra charge for full-coverage insurance (that is, to eliminate any problems with minor damage to the vehicle). You must produce a valid driver's license -in practice, this is accepted without the **International Driver's License.** Do volunteer the names of all individuals who may be driving the vehicle. And during the main tourist season, make your reservation as far in advance as possible.

CHARTER CRUISES: This has become a most popular way of visiting the **Greek islands.** Cruises vary from 2 days to a week or longer, and sometimes include stops at other **Mediterranean ports** (e.g. **Ephesus** or **Constantinople** in **Turkey**). They are not especially cheap, but considering that you save on hotel rooms and have to eat someplace, and that the alternatives (less comfortable small interisland ships or expensive airplanes) do not appeal to many people, these cruises become the best choice for many people. The principal disadvantage is the short time allowed on shore in most cases. Most of these cruises originate in **Athens-Piraeus,** but inquire at any travel agent for information.

CHURCHES: Since about 98% of all Greeks belong to the Greek Orthodox Church, it is not surprising that most churches will be of that faith. Visitors to Greece should make a point of stepping into some of these churches, whether old or new, large or small; best time is when a service is being held-even better when some special holy day or occasion such as a wedding or baptism is being celebrated. (Greeks are happy to see foreigners in attendance.) It used to be possible to step into any remote chapel, but with an increase of thefts of ikons and valuables in recent years, many chapels are now kept locked; usually the key is held by the priest or someone else in the nearest village. There are small pockets of **Roman Catholics in Greece** - in the **Ionian, Dodecannese,** and **Cycladic islands,** and of course a large foreign community in Athens - and services are held in their own churches. There are relatively few **Protestants in Greece,** and most of these are foreigners in **Athens,** where there are several **Protestant churches.** There are also Jewish synagogues in **Athens** and **Thessaloniki.**

CIGARETTES and CIGARS: Greeks continue to smoke cigarettes as though cancer had never been invented. The Greek cigarettes (and they grow a great deal of tobacco) come in all strengths and prices, and determined smokers should be able to find a brand to substitute for their otherwise very expensive favorites from home. There are limits on how many can be imported free of duty into Greece: 200 cigarettes, 50 cigars (or 200 grams of tobacco for a pipe).

CLOTHING: If you come during the hot months-May through September-you can get by in most situations with a light wardrobe. Do bring at least a sweater for cool evenings, however. And of course if you intend to spend time at higher elevations, you must bring adequate clothing-for cooler weather, possible rain, and any special requirements (such as rugged shoes for hiking). Greeks are informal dressers, and at beaches almost anything goes; however, they do not like to see people wearing beachwear in towns or in stores away from the beach; villagers are especially conservative, and you will create unnecessary comments if you parade around villages in scanty beachwear. You can always buy needed clothing in Greece, but it is not especially cheap. There are some local specialties, of course-informal shirts, shawls or sweaters, sandals, sunhats, etc.

COMPLAINTS: With literally millions of foreigners moving around Greece each year, it is impossible not to have occasional incidents or cases of dissatisfaction. Many of these arise from language problems or cultural differences. But if you feel you have a legitimate complaint, there are several possibilities. Start with the local **Tourist Police** or **National Tourist Organization office:** the emergency **phone number** for the **Tourist Police** all over Greece is **171.** Athens has a special number for handling complaints by foreigners: **135.** One way to stop possible episodes is to ask for 77 an itemized bill or receipt that you can indicate you intend to show to the **Tourist Police.**

CONSULATES and EMBASSIES: All the major nations of the world maintain embassies in Athens, but most travelers are more apt to need help in some more remote city. Many countries maintain consulates in other Greek cities-and often in unexpected cities, due to levels of commerce or tourism in these areas. Many of these consuls are local nationals, but they are authorized to help. Likewise, even if your own country does not maintain a consulate in a particular city, another country's might be able to help if it primarily a matter-at least at the outset-of finding someone who speaks your language. (Example: You need someone to translate a Greek document.)

CREDIT CARDS: The major international and certain national credit cards are accepted in many situations around Greece. The expected scale of acceptance prevails: the more expensive and more internationally-oriented the facility (hotel, restaurant, store), the more likely they are to honor credit cards. You cannot expect small tavernas, little pensions, village shops, to honor such cards. In most cases, those places that honor credit cards display plaques or signs so indicating at the front. And in the case of car rentals, credit cards are actually preferred for they serve to assure the agencies of your credit standing. See also TRAVELERS CHECKS

CUSTOMS CONTROL: For the mass of foreigners who visit Greece, customs control is so relaxed that it will hardly be noticed. You will have to pass through passport and customs control on your first point of entry into Greece-for most people, this will mean **Athens, Piraeus,** or one of the border checkpoints at the north, or **Patras.** There are some limits, however, and although you might slip in uninspected, you should know of these. You can bring in unlimited sums of travellers checks or foreign currency, but you are limited to bringing in (and taking out) 1,500 Drachmas. Only 200 cigarettes or 50 cigars or 200 grams of tobacco can be brought in; 1 liter of liquor or 1 liter of wine may be imported. Cameras, typewriters, radios, tape-recorders may be brought in as long as they are clearly for personal use; there are some limits on weapons and you should inquire before setting out for Greece. You cannot import explosives or narcotics (or parrots!). In leaving, you are limited to how much olive oil you can take out tax-free (as well as to 1,500 Drachmas and antiques-before 1830-and antiquities without official permission: See ANTIQUITIES).

DENTISTS: Dentists are to be found in all large to middle-sized cities. Most have trained abroad (and so will speak at least one foreign language) and they will usually have quite modern equipment. Their rates should be quite reasonable. When in need of a dentist, start by asking at the hotel reception desk (especially at the better grade hotels) or the **Tourist Police:** for one thing, someone can then phone ahead and explain your problem.

DOCTORS: Doctors are found in all large to middle-sized cities, although various specialists may be found only in the former. Most of these doctors will have done some of their studies abroad and so will speak at least one foreign language. Their knowledge, equipment, and techniques will be thoroughly up to date. In **Athens** especially, you must expect to pay international rates; elsewhere doctors may be somewhat cheaper. Incidentally, if you had a medical emergency in a small or remote locale, the local people would certainly help in getting a doctor to you or you to a doctor. See also PHARMACIES.

DRIVING IN GREECE: Large numbers of foreigners now drive either their own or rented vehicles around Greece. In both cases you need a **valid driver's licence,** and theoretically you should have an **International Driver's License.** It if it is your own car you are bringing into Greece, you need its registration (or log book) and you need proof of adequate insurance. There will be limits (usually about 4 months) on the length of time you can drive your car in Greece; you can usually get an extension (for 8 months) to continue driving your car without any major registration fees. The car will be entered in your passport, so if you were for any reason want to sell it in Greece, you must make very sure you are in full compliance with Greek laws governing such transactions.

Your car-and all rented vehicles - are exempt from the Greek law governing alternate Sunday regulations (even number plates-odd number plates). But foreigners must obey speed limits (and police can demand payment of fines on the spot) and you should observe parking regulations: the Greek custom is for police to remove license plates-and then force you to go around to a police station to pay the fine to get your plates back!

Fuel of all grades is available all over Greece-at some of the highest rates in the world. Because almost all Greeks drive imported cars (some foreign vehicles are now being assembled in Greece), there is no problem obtaining spare parts or experienced repairmen for your vehicle. (You may be amazed at the age of some of the boys who work on your vehicle-under adult supervision, you hope.)

Driving is on the right. Roads are not always well marked for danger spots or unusual conditions: curves, soft shoulders, fallen rocks, steep gradients-these are often not indicated. And although Greece has built up an impressive national highway system, many roads are in need of basic maintenance: it is not uncommon to encounter major potholes or rough stretches in the middle of otherwise decent highways. In addition, Greek drivers themselves retain a few habits from the days before motor vehicles were so common: they turn into main highways, stop along the road without warning, weave in and out in city streets. (Greece has one of the highest fatality rates from driving accidents.) But with basic caution, you should have no trouble driving in Greece. 79

DRUGS: Greek authorities take a very strict approach on importing drugs. On the other hand, Greek men in certain locales do smoke marijuana and use even stronger drugs. But foreigners would be advised to have nothing to do with drugs while in Greece.

DRYCLEANING: There are plenty of drycleaning establishments in all large to medium-sized cities. It is relatively cheap and fast-you should be able to get your clothing back within the day if you bring it early and make your needs clear. See also LAUNDRY.

EARTHQUAKES: Despite the publicity that attends earthquakes in Greece-from the days of **Lost Atlantis** to the ones that struck the **Athens area** in 1980 – these need not be of concern to visitors. The odds are that the most anyone will experience might be a slight tremor. One might just as well stay away from **Italy**-or **California,** for that matter.

EASTER: In many respects, **Easter** is the major occasion of the Greek year. Many Foreigners deliberately time their visit to Greece so as to be able to experience some of the events associated with the **Greek Easter.** Because it does not usually coincide with the **Easter** celebrated in the **Western Christian churches,** care must be taken that you do not arrive at the wrong time. The **Greek Orthodox Easter** is calculated as follows: it must fall after the first full moon following the first day of spring (as is true with **Western Christian Easter**) but it must also fall after the **Jewish Passover.** This then affects the **Lent** period-including the two weeks before **Lent** known as Carnival, with its festivities and parades, culminating in **Clean Monday,** with its vegetarian feast and kite-flying. And of course **Good Friday** depends on Easter's date: this is marked by a funeral procession through the streets. Saturday evening involves a church service that ends at midnight with the lighting of candles. **Easter Sunday** itself is an occasion for feasting and festivities. And even the Monday after is observed as a holiday. Ideally you should try to get invited to some village where the traditional **Easter** is observed, but even in the large cities there is enough to make a stranger feel the full impact of Easter on Greeks.

ELECTRICITY: Greece has now converted to A(lternating) C(urrent) at 220 voltage. This means that **Americans** must have converters for their 110-115 volt electrical appliances. Furthermore Greek outlets and plugs vary considerably from both **American** and many **European** standard types, so converters may be required. But electricity is virtually everywhere in Greece.

EMBASSIES: See CONSULATES AND EMBASSIES

EMERGENCIES: For emergency help of any kind, you will get a response 24 hours a day (and hopefully in a language you can speak) by dialing either the **Tourist Police** **(171)** or the regular police, **(100)** anywhere in Greece. (However, in smaller towns and villages, you will first have to dial the code to the nearest large city). Another possibility is to get to a hotel's reception desk and ask them to make the first call.

FISHING: There is relatively little freshwater fishing in most parts of Greece-and the saltwater fishing in the Mediterranean is not as good as one might assume. But Greeks do catch fish, obviously. No license is required. Nor is any license required for underwater speargun fishing: however, you must be at least 200 meters (667 feet) away from any other people in the water.

FOOD AND DRINK: Whatever else people come to Greece to enjoy, they all spend a fair amount of their time in eating and drinking. And since food and drink end up being among the main ingredients-and usually pleasures-of a Greek holiday, certain things might be said to improve their chances of being enjoyed.

To start with the first meal, breakfast-in most hotels this will be the "continental" type: coffee, possibly some sort of juice, bread, butter, and jelly. Unfortunately, all too often these are less than exciting. If you are required to take breakfast as part of your hotel's rates, that's that. But if you have a choice, you might consider going out and assembling your own breakfast: buying fresh fruit, buying your own roll or cheese pie or sweet, and then taking nothing but coffee in a cafe. Depending on your personal preference, you can take your large dinner at noon or in the evening, as most Greek restaurants offer the same menu, noon and night. (Only the more luxurious restaurants prepare a more elaborate menu for the even-

ing.) But consider: if you intend to move about in the heat of the afternoon, you should probably eat light. Then treat yourself to something refreshing late afternoon. For Greeks eat their evening meal late-anything before 8 PM is considered early. Another variation is to assemble your own picnic for the noon meal-fresh fruits, bread, cheeses, sliced meats or sardines, etc. And when ordering meals in restaurants, you are welcome to go back to the kitchen area to inspect and point out exactly what you want (and don't hesitate to send back anything that is not what you want). If you do not care for much olive oil, indicate that you want little or no **ladhi**. And if you find the food tepid to cold, indicate that you want your food served **zestós**. (If you're lucky, they'll get it as hot as you prefer it).

Greeks like to eat snacks when drinking anything alcoholic. Shrimp, tomato slices, bits of cheese, artichoke leaves - these are known as **mezés** or **mezedákis**; similar hors d'oeuvres as part of a full meal are **orektiká**. **Mezés** can be had at almost any little cafe or snack place. Sweets and ice cream (**pagotá**) are obtained at special sweethshops and cafés. Traditionally, Greeks go to these places for desserts, which are not available at typical restaurants.

Coffee was not traditionally served at restaurants, either, but now, to satisfy their many foreign patrons, some restaurants have taken to serving coffee. You must specify whether you want **ellenikós kafés** or "American" (or "French") coffee; the latter will usually be powdered coffee, while the former is what is widely known abroad as the Turkish style-a small cup with the muddy coffee taking up about the bottom third of the cup. The sugar is boiled with the coffee and you must specify the degree of sweetness you want: medium is **métrios,** sweet in **glykó,** light is **me olighi,** and no sugar at all is **skétos.** Tea is avialable, too. And Greeks usually take a glass of cold water with everything they eat or dring. Beer is a popular drink-there are several brands brewed in Greece that are quite decent. As for wines, the native Greek wines certainly can't compete with the world's better varieties, but some are adequate. There is first of all a choice between the **retsina**-wines that have been stored in "resinated" barrels and thus have a mild turpentine(!) flavor: not to everyone's taste, but in fact they go well with the Greek menu-and the **aretsinoto** wines. In addition to the usual whites, pinks, and reds, there are sweet dessert wines and quite good Greek brandies. There is also the Greek **oúzo,** made from distilling the crushed mash after the juice has been pressed from the grapes and then adding a slight anisette flavor.

Above all, whether eating or drinking, in fancy restaurants or simple tavernas, everyone should occasionally experiment with some of the different items on the Greek menu. Don't stay in the rut with the same **moussaká** and Greek salad.

See also RESTAURANTS.

GREEK LANGUAGE: The Greek language is far too complex and subtle to even begin to be taught or learned in a book like this. But there are a few basics that can be conveyed. Elsewhere (pages 94) a short list of words and phrases are provided to help the traveler in the more common situations.

The Written language: Most visitors to Greece will have little to do with written Greek except to attempt to read signs, menus, etc. Greek pronunciation is difficult enough so that its finer points could involve long discussions. Here is the alphabet with the English equivalent of the most common sounds so that at least a start can be made on reading Greek.

The Spoken language: Acquiring even the most basic spoken Greek is difficult or not, depending on an individual's skill in picking up a foreign language. But because of the unfamiliar alphabet, many foreigners get easily discouraged: there is not that gratuitous gain that comes from just looking at words in some foreign languages and gradually realizing that you can figure out meanings. Yet anyone should be able to rely on their ear and then try to approximate pronunciations. Greeks are genuinely appreciative of any such efforts. One problem, however, that Greeks have ignoring: their language depends so much on the accent's falling on the precise syllable that this becomes at least as important as the purity of the sound. When in doubt, try shifting the accent until you hit the proper syllable.

The casual traveler need not become concerned about the

historical rivalries between the "pure" and demotic spoken Greek: the demotic will be fine for all situations. Likewise, although there are numerous dialects spoken in various parts of Greece-some quite different in pronunciation and vocabulary-the foreigner will be doing fine just to speak a basic Greek. Put another way, dialect variations are the least of a foreigner's problems!

GUIDES AND INTERPRETERS: Officially licensed guides can be provided from the **National Tourist Organization offices** or by the bigger travel agents. Their fees are also officially controlled-and depend on such factors as the time involved, the number in the party, the difficulty of the excursion, etc. Tours organized by travel agencies, of course, usually provide guides who speak the language(s) of the majority of the foreigners taking the tour. If you are lucky, you will get a guide who

HAIRDRESSERS: There are many hairdressers in all large to medium-sized Greek cities. You can get a complete line of services. Tipping is expected-perhaps 10% for the principal hairdresser, half that for the assistant.

HITCHHIKING: As long as basic precautions are observed, hitchhiking (also known to Europeans as "autostop") is generally allowed throughout Greece. Young women, whether alone or in pairs, should exercise special judgment as to the rides they accept.

HOLIDAYS: There are two types of holidays that tourists will want to know about while in Greece. One includes the national holidays when not only all banks, museums, archaeological sites, almost all stores, and even many restaurants are closed. These are the following days:

January 1-	New Year's day
January 6-	Epifhany
Last Monday before Lent	
Good Friday	
Easter Sunday	Movable dates (**See** EASTER)
Easter Monday	
March 25	Greek Independence Day
May 1	Spring Festival, or May Day
August 15-	Assumption of the Virgin Mary
October 28-	Okhi (No!) Day
	(Second World War incident)
December 25-	Christmas Day

not only is comfortable with your language but has a true command of the subject-that is, you will get much more than a mechanical-rote recitation of facts.

But it addition to these national holidays, there are numerous local holidays and festivals-in honor of some historical or patriotic event, a saint, an age-old festival. In

83

particular, "name-days" are major occasions when the saint's name is one of the more popular ones: people with that name often come from great distances to a monastery, chapel, or village where that saint is especially honored. Sometimes Greek festivities go on for two or more days, involving dancing and feasting. Foreigners are traditionally welcomed, and anyone with a taste for such occasions should inquire from the **National Tourist Organization office** or **Tourist Police** - or, for that matter, from almost any Greek who seems informed-about any forthcoming holiday of this kind. See also HOURS, EASTER.

HOSPITALITY: Greek hospitality is legendary, and it usually lives up to its reputation, especially in more remote villages and where only a few foreigners are involved. But in recent years, with the influx of literally millions of foreigners annually, there has inevitably been some pulling back: there is no way that Greeks can "relate to" every single foreigner who crosses paths with them, let alone afford to extend the full panoply of traditional hospitality. However, arrive in a small party in a remote village and you may still be treated as a special guest-offered special drinks and food, presented with little gifts when you leave. Greek males still usually insist on paying for meals when they take a foreigner to a favorite eating place. You will often be offered a coffee or cold drink when visiting with a Greek-and the Greeks present will expect you to accept even as they refuse anything for themselves. But this hospitality works both ways. Greeks in these situations will often question foreigners about fairly personal matters-why a married couple doesn't have children, how much money you have paid for certain items. And once the preliminaries are underway, Greeks expect you to participate to the end: if they have begun to plan a meal for you, they would be genuinely hurt if you ran off to save them the trouble and expense. So don't embark on these encounters unless you are prepared to enjoy them all the way.

HOSPITALS: All large, medium-sized, and even some quite small towns have hospitals or at least clinics. You might go direct to one if you have some medical emergency. Only in the larger cities, of course, could you expect to find a full range of services and specialists. Greek hospitals provide minimal nursing care: a member of the family will often bed down next to the patient to provide full attention, meals, etc. Most foreigners will never have any contact with hospitals, but if you had to you will find that they are quite adequate. See also DOCTORS, EMERGENCIES.

HOSTELS: There are **Youth Hostels** throughout Greece - in most major cities and also in tourist centers. You will almost certainly be asked to produce a membership card from a recognized Youth Hostel association; if you do not have one from your home country, you can join (for a fee) the **Greek Youth Hostels Association** (at 4 Dragatsaniou

84

Street, Athens). There is usually a limit of 5 days on your stay at these hostels.

HOTELS: There are hotels to suit all tastes and all pocketbooks all over Greece. If you have particular preferences as to price, location, or other specifics, you should reserve in advance for the main tourist season: no one ever spends the night on the street, but you cannot be certain of getting the exact hotel you want. At other times of the year, however, there is generally a surplus of beds. All hotel and room accommodations in Greece are quite strictly controlled-as to price, conditions, etc.-by the government. There are various classes, or categories, of hotels, form Deluxe and then Class A through E; the criteria may not always seem important to all guests (e.g. size of public rooms, telephones in rooms), but in general the categories reflect the levels of amenities. Many tourists find the Class C hotels-most of which are relatively new-quite adequate (and they cost about one-half a Class A hotel and two-thirds a Class B). The prices are supposed to be posted in each room, but sometimes it is hard for a hotel to keep up with all seasonal changes.

Ask for the price of the room before you agree to anything (and then ask to inspect it , if you care to). Find out if the price quoted includes all taxes and whether it includes any meals: hotels are allowed to require clients to take breakfast, if offered by the hotel, and the Class B, A, and Deluxe hotels may also require clients to take at least one other meal if the hotel maintains a dining room. Service charges should be included in the price quoted, but you may want to tip a bit extra anyone who has done you any personal favors. Prices may be raised during the "high" tourist season (and may be lowered during the off season); hotels can also charge an extra 10% if you stay less than three nights. It all sounds quite complicated, but in practice you are told a price of a room and that's usually the end of it. Do clarify the various possibilities, however, if you are concerned.

HOURS: Greek shop hours can be a quite complicated subject, but in general stores open at 8 AM and close around 1:30 or 2 PM, Monday through Saturday; on several days a week (but not Saturday) some shops reopen again from about 5 to 8:30 PM. Inquire in the morning if you have any special needs for that day. And of course all shops observe the national holidays. See HOLIDAYS.

HUNTING: Foreigners may hunt within Greece but only with a license and with limitations on seasons, type of game, etc. There are also limits on the types of weapons and ammunition you can bring in. Inquire at the **National Tourist Organization** or a **Greek Embassy** abroad if this is to be an important part of your visit to Greece.

INFORMATION: There are various sources for detailed information about Greece. Abroad, there are the **Greek Embassies** and **Consulates;** the **National Tourist Organization** maintains offices in many of the principal cities of the world; and travel agents have some types of touristic information. Within Greece, there are the various offices of the **National Tourist Organization,** the **Tourist Police,** and also the travel agencies. One of the problems for all of these offices is to keep up with the many changes from year to year and from season to season in schedules, prices, etc. Thus, not until you actually get to Greece can you probably find out exact times and costs of the sailings to the many Greek islands; what you should be able to learn while still abroad is whether such service is usually available.

LAUNDRY: Laundry can usually be placed at a drycleaning establishment to be picked up within 24 hours, and the better class hotels usually will take care of laundry for their clients. But wherever it is done, it will seem expensive (especially relative to so many other costs in Greece). But every item will be neatly ironed, and in some situations this service may be a necessary expense. There are almost no self-service laundries anywhere in Greece-there has been one in the **Plaka** section of **Athens.** Most tourists simply make do by washing out things in their rooms and then hanging them on the usually present balcony.

LUGGAGE: Greek air terminals and bus stations usually do not provide any place to leave luggage for even short periods of time. Tourists are left to make their own arrangements-with a cafe, restaurant, hotel, store, or wherever. Offer a reasonable sum for the

service, and although it cannot be legally guaranteed, your luggage should always be safe.

MEDICINES: See PHARMACIES

MENU: See RESTAURANTS

MONEY: The basic Greek currency is the Drachma. The Lepta-100 make up a Drachma-has all but vanished from common usage, although occasionally prices are quoted with a 50 Lepta. (When Greek shopkeepers or others lack small change, they automatically "round off"-sometimes to your advantage, sometimes to theirs). The exchange rate of the Drachma with various foreign currencies has been fluctuating so in recent years that it would be misleading to provide specific figures here. As soon as you find out the exchange rate for your own national currency, calculate some basic equivalencies-that is, what does 5 Drachmas, equal, 10 Drachmas, 50 Drachmas, etc. This will provide a general sense of what things are costing. Technically you are limited to importing (and exporting) 1,500 Drachmas in currency; most foreigners are never even questioned, let alone inspected, but there is no real "black market" in Greek currency and little opportunity for most people to gain anything by violating the law. See also BANKS.

MOTORBIKES FOR RENT: Motorbikes may be rented from various agents in the main cities and resort centers. Rates vary but they obviously become cheaper over longer periods. During the main tourist season and over holidays, you should probably reserve in advance. To rent a motorbike, however, you must be at least 18 years of age and licensed to operate one. You (and any passengers) must wear a protective helmet. And you should carry all the insurance you can get. See also BICYCLES FOR RENT.

MOUNTAINEERING: It may be overlooked-considering that most people come to Greece to enjoy the beaches and water-that Greece also has many fine mountains that offer challenging and enjoyable possibilities. There is a **Greek Mountainclimbing Club** (EOS is the Greek acronym), with branches in many cities, and foreigners are made to feel welcome on their excursions and in their facilities. They maintain various huts on major mountains. Although the peaks may not seem that high by world standards, the weather conditions often make some of the ascents quite difficult, and certainly no one should set out to climb unless properly equipped and experienced. Consult the **National Tourist Organization** for details about contacting a local mountaineering club or obtaining a local guide.

MOVIES: No one would ever travel to Greece to see a movie-the selection, even in **Athens,** is usually dismal, and in smaller cities it is hard to know where such movies have come from. But there are times when someone might want to retreat to a movie, and during the summer, when there are many outdoor movie theaters, it can be quite pleasant to sit under the starry Mediterranean sky and sit back and enjoy a movie you'd feel guilty about

seeing at home. Most foreign films in Greece are shown in their original language and with Greek subtitles, but ask to make sure before you enter.

NEWSPAPERS AND MAGAZINES: There is a large selection of foreign-language (that is, non-Greek) newspapers and magazines to be found in the large and medium-sized cities and also in all tourist centers. Athens has an English-language daily, **The Athens News,** and a fine English-language monthly, **The Athenian.** There is also a good selection of papers and periodicals brought in from abroad; they tend to be expensive (compared to prices at home) and the news will seem a bit dated (when you first arrive), but the longer you stay the more you may appreciate these links with the world.

PARKING: There was once a time when there were so few cars that finding a parking place was no problem in Greece. Then came a phase when the car population "exploded" so fast they took over every available sidewalk and corner. Now the Greek police have begun to fight back: in Athens and some cities, the police remove the license plates when your car is in violation and you must go to the local stationhouse and pay the fine to retrieve your plates. Meters are appearing in some cities. Parking restrictions are generally enforced, for foreigners as well as Greeks. Athens and several other cities and tourist centers have set aside a few places for tourist parking (marked by signs) but during the main season these are as hard to find free as any other places.

PASSPORTS AND VISAS: A valid national passport is all that is required of most visitors to Greece-although you will probably be asked to fill out an entry card on the airplane or ship-so long as you are a transient: This period varies (depending on reciprocal arrangements with the individual's home country), but for **British** and **Commonwealth** subjects this is three months and for **Americans,** two months. For longer stays, visas must be applied for: Inquire at the **Tourist Police** or **National Tourist Organization** as to how to proceed.

PENSIONS: These are a cheaper, more basic type of accommodation to be found in locales where a lot of travelers pass through. You probably won't have a private toilet or bath, and the buildings will usually be older, but linen will be clean and some people prefer the more homey atmosphere. Breakfast is usually available at a pension. See also ROOMS TO RENT.

PHARMACIES: Pharmacies, drugstores, or chemists, there are plenty of them around Greece and they carry a fairly full selection of prescription drugs as well as general health, sanitary, and cosmetic items. (A pharmacy is usually clearly marked by a **red Maltese cross.**) There will always be at least one pharmacy open, 24 hours a day, in any large city: the closed ones should have a sign in their window indicating which one is open. If you have special medical needs, of course, you had better make arrangements with your own doctor at home before setting off.

PHOTOGRAPHY: Greece is famed as a photographer's paradise, what with its light and subjects. There are plenty of shops selling films and camera supplies-but all are expensive and you are advised to bring your own. You can get your films developed in relatively short times. In traveling about Greece, be careful to observe the occasional restrictions against photographing in areas of military bases.

POLICE: See EMERGENCIES

POST OFFICE: Any good-sized city will have its post office, and larger cities will have several branch offices. They keep varied hours, but best is to get there in the morning. Some will open for only limited service in the late afternoon-postage stamps or for **Poste Restante.** (This latter refers to mail addressed to someone with no other known or fixed address-what Americans know as **General Delivery.**) Postage rates vary considerably (and rise inevitably) depending on the nature of the item (post card, letter, etc.), the weight, the destination, etc. The best is to know the basic stamps for most of your mail (that is, air mail post cards to your homeland, the lightest air mail letters, etc.) and be prepared to have any mail in question weighed. Stamps can often be purchased at certain stationery shops but you will pay a slight surcharge for the privilege.

PRICES: The one thing certain is that they will rise over time, in Greece as elsewhere. Some prices, however, do come down during the off-season-hotels in particular. By and large, prices are well marked for most items you will be purchasing, whether food in the market, or clothes in a store, and Greeks do not appreciate your trying to negotiate prices. If a shopkeeper sees you about to leave he may make some kind of a reduction or offer, but he does not want you to turn every purchase into a bazaar haggling.

RADIO: There are several possibilities for foreigners who like to keep up with the news via radio and in their own language. Greek stations provide at least one brief program daily with news and weather in **English, French,** and **German.** The American Armed Forces Radio broadcasts 24 hours daily, with frequent news updates. And there is the **BBC** overseas and the **Voice of America.**

REDUCTIONS: There are some reductions in admissions to museums and archaeological sites but they are limited to special groups. Foreign students of subjects directly related to the world of Greek art and archaeology can get a pass that allows for a 50% reduction to all national sites and museums (not to locally run). Students who present an **International Student Identity Card** are granted a reduced fee at some places. And a very special group of archaeologists, professors of art and architecture and classical subjects, museum professionals, **UNESCO** and some other government officials are given free entry to sites and muse-

ums. If you think you qualify, go to the **Directorate of Antiquities,** 14 Aristidou St., Athens, with proper identification and find out how to comply.

RELIGION: See CHURCHES

RESTAURANTS: There is no problem in finding a restaurant in Greece, and although they range from the quite elaborate and expensive to the rather dingy and cheap, most foreigners end up patronizing a relatively narrow spectrum. They are officially classed, and this affects the prices they are allowed to charge. The easy way to approach a restaurant is to make sure its appearance appeals and then look at some standard item on the menu-which should always be posted out front-and see how its price compares with the same item in other places you've eaten in. Not necessarily, but usually, if the moussaka or Greek salad is expensive, then everything will be expensive. Once you have decided to eat there, go to the kitchen area and select your foods-most proprietors are happy to have you do so; this eliminates the need for a lot of talking and the possibility of some unwanted surprises. Send back food if it is not what you want. The standard printed Greek menu has its prices listed in two columns: that on the left is the price before the obligatory service charge, that on the right includes the service percentage-and it is the latter you will be billed for. It is customary, even so, to tell the waiter to keep a small extra sum when he presents the change; and if there was a "waterboy"for your table you leave a few Drachmas for him.

ROOMS TO RENT: In some of the more crowded tourist centers individual families have taken to renting rooms in their homes. They are supposed to be supervised so that basic sanitary practices are observed, no matter how simple the accommodation. They are relatively cheap and many people find such rooms adequate. See also PENSIONS

SAILING: See YACHTS

SHOESHINE: In the larger cities, young boys or even men will be shining shoes in various public areas. Agree on the price beforehand-and if you are in doubt, ask a Greek to help establish the cost. A small tip is customary.

SHOPPING AND SOU-VENIRS: In the largest and even in relatively small cities of Greece, you will be able to purchase almost any item you need for your stay in Greece. Often as not it will even be your favorite brand, since Greeks import virtually everything: your favorite suntan lotion, your preferred instant coffee-they'll probably be available. But these are not what most people come to Greece to buy. It is the souvenirs and specialties of Greece that interest most travelers, and here the selection is almost overwhelming, especially in the major tourist centers. Since everyone's taste differs as to what constitutes a suitable souvenir, there is no use laying down rules. Take your time and look around: it is not that shops cheat but simply that prices often will be lower in one place than another-and sometimes the lowest price will be in some unexpected location. (Even then, the difference may be relatively few Drachmas, so you must ask yourself how much of your limited time you want to spend in comparison shopping.) It is difficult to find genuine handmade artifacts, but they are available, and often not that much more expensive than the massproduced items. Often it is the smaller and less centrally located shops that have the unusual items, so leave the main streets lined with gift shops and go looking. Even then, don't give too much credence to claims of age or uniqueness or "the last one left...": just buy what you like at the price you feel you want to pay. See also PRICES and HOURS.

SPORTS: Those who like to include active sports in their vacations and travels will find many opportunities to do so in Greece. In the winter, for instance, there are several ski lifts operating (most of them in central and northern Greece, but one in the White Mountains of Crete). There are several golf clubs in Greece (near **Athens,** and on **Rhodes** and **Corfu**). There is horseback riding (at Athens, Salonica, and on Crete). Several of the major resort hotels offer waterskiing, and many public beaches now have paddleboats and surfsails for rent. And Greek youths can usually be found playing informal games of soccer (football) or basketball: if you ask, you could probably join in. See also Mountaineering, Swimming, Tennis, Underwater Sports, Yachting.

SWIMMING: Swimming-or at least sunbathing is perhaps the main attraction for many visitors to Greece, and there are almost limitless beaches. In fact, though, not all Greek beaches are as sandy as you might wish. Inquire if you have a strong preference and a choice as to where the sandy beach is located. Likewise, not all beaches are as clean as you might wish-although if you get away from a city or built-up area the water should be perfectly clean and clear. What you cannot always escape-anywhere in the Mediterranean - is the tar that washes ashore and gets into the sand: a beach may look perfectly clean. but as you walk along the sand your feet pick up the buried tar. (This is one reason many people have taken to bringing flexible mats to the beaches: to save their towels from getting fouled). The usual precautions about avoiding undertows and un-expected currents should be observed. Many cities operate public beach facilities-changing rooms, showers, etc. Nudist beaches are officially forbidden and in some areas local individuals actively seek to enforce the ban; in some places, if it is done with discretion, it will be ignored. Lastly the Mediterranean is not the tropics, and most people find the swimming season lasts only from May through September.

TAXIS: Taxis remain relatively cheap in Greece. They can also be hard to hire during certain busy hours-and for that reason, Greeks often share taxis, each party paying the metered fare to their destination. There is a minimum fare, too-no matter how short the distance. There may also be some surcharges beyond the metered fare: for night rides, for certain holidays, for luggage, to airports, etc. (Drivers should be able to indicate any such surcharges.) If it is to be an especially long trip, negotiate the fee before leaving. If it is to a remote locale and you want the driver to wait, there are set fees for waiting time. With two or more individuals sharing the cost, a taxi offers a reasonable way to make best use of a limited time in Greece.

TELEPHONES AND TELEGRAMS: In a few large cities, it has been traditional to use the phones available at many kiosks (or **peripterons**); you dial first and after you have completed your call you pay the proprietor. Now a large red telephone is replacing this system-and you must insert the coin first (it has for some time been a two-Drachma coin). Increasingly, too, phone booths are appearing all over Greece, and for these you need a two - Drachma coin. In some special phone booths you can even dial long distance, but most foreigners (as do most Greeks) will prefer to go to the office of the national phone company (**OTE**) and use the attended services. If you know-or can learn-the code numbers for your desired call, you can dial direct to virtually any place in the world. (Be persistent, though: the Greek phone system is good, but you must often try dialing several times to make your connection. When you are finished with your call, you step over to the attendant who will read the meter and provide you with a "bill". Since many Greeks still do not have telephones, these offices can be quite crowded at certain times, so go well in advance if you must place a call within a set period. Telegrams are sent from these same offices. The forms are printed in English as well as Greek, and the attendants are usually adept at dealing with foreigners' queries. Large hotels might be able to help you, too, with any special problems.

TENNIS: There are a fair number of tennis courts around Greece and most are open to non-Greeks (and non-members of the sponsoring clubs). Naturally the courts tend to be concentrated in a few areas-Athens (and its nearby beach resorts), large cities such as **Salonika** and **Patras,** and in the more popular holiday centers such as Crete, Rhodes, and Corfu. Inquire at offices of the **National Tourist Organization** for details; if tennis is a vital part of your holiday in Greece, you should make certain of arrangements before going to a particular locale.

THEFT: This is virtually a non-existent problem in Greece. Luggage can be left unattanded almost anywhere, purses or cameras can be forgotten at a restaurant-you will always find them waiting for you. On the other hand, it would be silly to leave a lot of currency or small valuables (jewels, watches, etc.) lying around in your hotel room: there are simply too many people passing through.

TIME: Greece is two hours ahead of **Greenwich Mean Time** (that is, **London's** time).

Greece now observes **Summer Time** (in which clocks are set one hour ahead) on the same schedule as its fellow **Common Market** members. As for time during the Greek day, Greeks do not concern themselves much with punctuality. Beyond that, when they say "tomorrow morning", they may mean at 12 noon; "this afternoon" may well mean 4 PM. Make a fixed appointment, by all means, but do not get excited if it isn't kept to the minute.

TIPPING: Greeks used to consider it as beneath their dignity to accept tips, but the influx of foreign tourists has changed all that. Even so, by including the service charges in restaurant bills and hotel bills, Greeks try to eliminate some of the awkwardness involved in tipping. It is customary to give the waiter at least some "rounded off" change (e.g. the 15 Drachmas over a 385 Drachma bill); coins left on the table will go to the waterboy if there has been one. If you have had some personal contact or asked special services of personnel in your hotel, it is certainly not out of line to present a tip. Barbers, hairdressers, shoes-hiners, and ushers (in movies as well as theaters) traditionally get modest tips. Taxi drivers are not supposed to expect tips, but you can expect a less than gracious smile if you do not at least give a small sum over the fare.

TOILETS: Hotels that most foreigners now stay in have modern toilet facilities (although the plumbing may look a bit exotic). Many of the older restaurants and tavernas, however, have quite primitive toilets: if you are squeamish about this, use your hotel toilet before going out to eat. There are public toilets (the attendants expect a tip) in all medium sized to large Greek cities-but they are often fairly primitive, too. Most of the better hotels have separate toilet facilities for their patrons, and if you look as though you belong you can usually make use of them.

TRAVELERS CHECKS: All the better known travelers checks are honored in banks, hotels, restaurants that cater to foreigners, and tourist gift shops. Do not expect every little corner store or village taverna, however, to accept a travelers check: buy your Drachmas before setting off for the countryside. See also CREDIT CARDS and BANKS.

UNDERWATER SPORTS: SCUBA diving is generally forbidden in Greek waters-the exception being in certain areas and under some supervision. (This restriction is because the Greeks fear that too many divers could lead to losses of their antiquities still to be found around the coasts.) Inquire at the National Tourist Organization for specifics. However, snorkeling (that is, with just a breathing tube, mask, and flippers) is allowed (as is fishing with a speargun, so long as it is not close to swimmers: See FISHING).

VILLAS FOR RENT: It is relatively easy-if expensive!-to rent completely furnished villas in many of the more popular holiday locales a-round Greece. (Villas, by the way, are distinguished from "houses" in that the former usually are out of the main residential areas and usually have a bit of land). Many villas are now rented only through various travel agents or firms specializing in such rentals: inquire of the National Tourist Organization or of major travel agents. Villas can be very expensive during the main season, but if several people are sharing the cost and make a fair number of meals at home, a villa can end up being relatively cheap.

VISAS: See PASSPORTS AND VISAS

WATER: The water of Greece is safe to drink in virtually any place the average traveler will be. (If foreigners sometimes complain of minor stomach ailments when traveling in Greece, it probably is not the water; in any case, it may be little more than a shift from one water to another-the type of upset one could experience in moving from any city to another). The fresh cold water from a natural spring is one of the delights of Greece. If you are truly sensitive, of course, you can always drink bottled water. A more realistic problem might be to get hot water whenever you want it in your hotel: ask beforehand to find out if hot water is provided at only certain hours.

YACHTING: There are numerous firms that rent yachts-mostly with crews - and this has become a popular way to tour Greece. They are undoubtedly expensive at first hearing, but if the cost is divided among several people, and then hotels, other transportation, and at least some meals are being eliminated, the end result is not that expensive. These yachts come in all sizes, with or without sail, and with greater or lesser degrees of luxury. Inquire of the National Tourist Organization or major travel agents for more details.

YOUTH HOSTELS: SEE HOSTELS

ZOOS: For those people who like to round out their view of a foreign land by visiting the local zoo, Greece offers nothing truly worthy of that name. Athens, however, does have a modest display of animals in the National Garden, and it offers the advantage of being central and a convenient retreat from the heat and bustle of the city. And many Greek cities maintain small collections of animals in their public parks-often including some of the less familiar species of Greece such as the famous wild goat of Crete. Inquire of the local **Tourist Police** if you enjoy such diversions.

5. A little Greek for travelers

A	α	(álfa)	As in far.
B	β	(víta)	Closer to a soft v than to b.
Γ	γ	(gámma)	Before a, o, u: **gh**. Before e, i: **y**.
Δ	δ	(dhélta)	Closer to **dh** than to hard **d**.
E	ε	(épsilon)	As in sell.
Z	ζ	(zíta)	As in zeal.
H	η	(íta)	As in machine.
Θ	θ	(thíta)	As in theater.
I	ι	(jóta)	As in machine.
K	κ	(káppa)	As in kit.
Λ	λ	(lámdha)	As in lamp.
M	μ	(mí)	As in mit.
N	ν	(ní)	As in not.
Ξ	ξ	(xí)	As **ks** sound (as in extra)
O	o	(ómikron)	As in oar.
Π	π	(pí)	As in pit.
P	ρ	(ró)	As in red.
Σ	σ ς	(sígma)	As in sit.
T	τ	(táf)	As in tap.
Y	υ	(ípsilon)	As in machine.
Φ	φ	(fí)	As in fish.
X	χ	(chí)	A **kh** sound (as in **Khan**).
Ψ	ψ	(psí)	A **ps** sound (as in **apse**).
Ω	ω	(oméga)	As in ode.

94

BASIC DAILY SITUATIONS

Yes	né
Yes indeed!	málista
No	óchi
Greetings!	chérete!
Good morning	kaliméra
Good evening	kalispéra
Good night	kaliníkta
Stay well!	sto kaló
Excuse me	me sinchoríte **or** signómi!
Please	parakaló
Thank you	efcharistó
Not at all	típota
How are you	Ti kánete? **or** pos páte?
Very well	polí kalá
Do you speak English?	Miláte angliká?
I don't understand	Dhen katalavéno
What is that called?	Pos to léne aftó?
How do you say that	Pos to léne aftó
in Greek?	sta ellhniká?
What is your name?	Pos sas léne?
My name is-	Me léne-
Mister	kírios
Mrs.	kiría
Child	pedhí
Much	polí
Little	lígho
Over	epáno
Under	káto
There	ekí
Here	edó
Big	megálos
Little	mikrós

NUMBERS

1	éna	18	dhekaoktó
2	dhio	19	dhekaenéa
3	tría	20	íkossi
4	téssara	21	ikosiéna
5	pénte	30	triánda
6	éxi	40	saránda
7	eftá	50	penínda
8	októ	60	exínda
9	enéa	70	evdomínta
10	dhéka	80	ogdhónda
11	éndheka	90	enenínda
12	dódheka	100	ekató
13	dhekatría	200	diakóssia

14	dhekatéssera	300	triakóssia
15	dhekapénde	1000	khília
16	dhekaéxi	2000	dhío khiliádes
17	dhekaeftá		

TIME

Morning	to proí
Midday	to messiméri
Afternoon	to apóyevma
Evening	to vrádhi
Night	i níkhta
Yesterday	chtés
Today	símera
Tomorrow	ávrio
Early	enorís
Late	argá
When?	Póte?
Four o'clock (AM)	Stis tésseres to proí
At 5:30 PM	Stis pendémisi to apóyevma
Sunday	Kiriakí
Monday	Dheftéra
Tuesday	Tríti
Wednesday	Tetárti
Thursday	Pémpti
Friday	Paraskeví
Saturday	Sávato
Hour	óra
Day	iméra
Week	evdhomádha
Month	mínas
Year	chrónos

HOTEL

Hotel	xenodhokhío
Room	dhomátio
Bathroom	bánio
Bed	kreváti
Cover	kouvérta
Pillow	maxilári
Lamp	lámba
Cold water	krío neró
Hot water	zestó neró
Key	klidhí
Guest	xénos
Do you have a room with 2 beds?	Échete éna dhíklino dhomátio?
I am staying only one night	Tha míno mía níkhta

| Can I pay with a credit card? | Boró na pliróso me aftí ti pistotikí kárta? |
| Do you accept travelers' checks? | Pérnete travellers checks? |

RESTAURANTS

Restaurant	estiatório
Food	fayitó
Table	trapézi
Chair	karékla
Napkin	petséta
Plate	piáto
Cup	flitzáni
Glass	potíri
Fork	piroúni
Spoon	koutáli
Knife	machéri
Waiter	garsóni
Waterboy	mikrós
Check	loghariasmós
Tip	pourboire
Menu	katáloghos
Hors d'oeuvres	orektiká
Bread	psomí
Water	neró
Wine	krassí
Beer	bíra
Milk	ghála
Meat	kréas
Fish	psária
Chicken	kotópoulo
Hot	zestós
Cold	kríos

AROUND TOWN

Street	othós
Square	platía
Boulevard	leofóros
Attention!	Prossochí!
Forbidden	Apaghorévete
Open	aniktós
Shut	klistós
Entrance	íssodhos
Exit	éxodhos
Toilet	toualéta
Women	ghynekón
Men	andhrón
Store	maghazí
Kiosk	períptero

Post office	takhidhromío
Letter	ghrámma
Stamp	grammatósimo
Airmail	aeroporikós
Telephone	tiléfono
Telegram	tilegráfima
How much does it cost?	Póso káni aftó?
Bank	trápeza
Money	khrímata
Drachmas	drachmés
I would like to exchange a check	Thélo na aláxo éna tsek.
Laundry	plidirio
Dry-cleaning	katharistírio
I need it tommorow	Prépi na íne étimo ávrio to proí

ON THE ROAD

Automobile	aftokínito
Bus	leoforío
Taxi	taxi
Motorcycle	motosikléta
Bicycle	podhílato
Ship	plío **or** karávi
Airplane	aeropláno
Railroad station	stathmós trénou
Stop(bus)	stássi
Map	khártis
Ticket	issitírio
Gas station	pratírion venzínis
Gas	venzíni
Oil	ládhi
Kilometer	khiliómetro
Straight ahead	kat efthían
Right	dhexiá
Left	aristerá
Opposite	apénandi
One way	apló
Roundtrip (return)	me epistrofí
Quickly	grígora
Slowly	sighá
Where is-?	Pou íne?-
How many hours?	Pósses óres?
When does the bus leave?	Ti óra févyi to leoforío?

INDEX

| Can I pay with a credit card? | Boró na plíróso me aftí ti pistotikí kárta? |
| Do you accept travelers' checks? | Pérnete travellers checks? |

RESTAURANTS

Restaurant	estiatório
Food	fayitó
Table	trapézi
Chair	karékla
Napkin	petséta
Plate	piáto
Cup	flitzáni
Glass	potíri
Fork	piroúni
Spoon	koutáli
Knife	machéri
Waiter	garsóni
Waterboy	mikrós
Check	loghariasmós
Tip	pourboire
Menu	katáloghos
Hors d'oeuvres	orektiká
Bread	psomí
Water	neró
Wine	krassí
Beer	bíra
Milk	ghála
Meat	kréas
Fish	psária
Chicken	kotópoulo
Hot	zestós
Cold	kríos

AROUND TOWN

Street	othós
Square	platía
Boulevard	leofóros
Attention!	Prossochí!
Forbidden	Apaghorévete
Open	aniktós
Shut	klistós
Entrance	íssodhos
Exit	éxodhos
Toilet	toualéta
Women	ghynekón
Men	andhrón
Store	maghazí
Kiosk	períptero

Post office	takhidhromío
Letter	ghrámma
Stamp	grammatósimo
Airmail	aeroporikós
Telephone	tiléfono
Telegram	tilegráfima
How much does it cost?	Póso káni aftó?
Bank	trápeza
Money	khrímata
Drachmas	drachmés
I would like to exchange a check	Thélo na aláxo éna tsek.
Laundry	plidirio
Dry-cleaning	katharistírio
I need it tommorow	Prépi na íne étimo ávrio to proí

ON THE ROAD

Automobile	aftokínito
Bus	leoforío
Taxi	taxi
Motorcycle	motosikléta
Bicycle	podhílato
Ship	plío **or** karávi
Airplane	aeropláno
Railroad station	stathmós trénou
Stop(bus)	stássi
Map	khártis
Ticket	issitírio
Gas station	pratírion venzínis
Gas	venzíni
Oil	ládhi
Kilometer	khiliómetro
Straight ahead	kat efthían
Right	dhexiá
Left	aristerá
Opposite	apénandi
One way	apló
Roundtrip (return)	me epistrofí
Quickly	grígora
Slowly	sighá
Where is-?	Pou íne?-
How many hours?	Pósses óres?
When does the bus leave?	Ti óra févyi to leoforío?

INDEX

99